A POCKET GU

THE
LITERATURE
OF WALES

A POCKET GUIDE

THE

LITERATURE

OF WALES

DAFYDD JOHNSTON

UNIVERSITY OF WALES PRESS
THE WESTERN MAIL

First published in 1994 by the University of Wales Press
Reprinted 1996
Reprinted in 1999 as a co-publication of the University of Wales Press and the Western Mail

ISBN 0-7083-1265-9

A catalogue record for this book is available from the British Library

Cover design by Chris Neale
Typeset in England by Create, Bath
Printed in Wales by Gwasg Dinefwr, Llandybïe

Contents

Preface

The main aim of this book is to provide essential factual information about the literature of Wales, both Welsh-language and English. But the very process of compression and selection inevitably goes further than that, involving subjective value-judgements. I have tried to be as even-handed as possible, but if my personal preferences are still obvious from the amount of space given to certain authors, then I can only hope that some degree of enthusiasm compensates for the loss in objectivity. As for the numerous excellent contemporary writers who have not been named, or not given their due, I can only plead lack of space and beg forgiveness. Unless otherwise stated, translations of extracts quoted are my own. I am aware that the historical background to the literature is only sketchily conveyed here, and would recommend J. Graham Jones's companion volume in this series on the history of Wales.

I would like to thank my colleagues, Dr Sioned Davies and Dr Medwin Hughes, for their helpful comments on parts of this book in typescript, and my wife, as ever, for her shrewd criticism. I am also indebted to Susan Jenkins and Ceinwen Jones of the University of Wales Press for their skilled editorial work.

DAFYDD JOHNSTON
July 1994

Acknowledgements

The author and publisher wish to thank the copyright holders who have kindly permitted the reproduction of the following:

Illustrations
The cover illustration is *Manawydan's Glass Door* (1931) by David Jones, reproduced by kind permission of the Trustees of David Jones. From a private collection.

Pages from the Book of Aneirin (p. 6), the Black Book of Carmarthen (p. 15), Peniarth 28 (p. 26), Peniarth 109 (p. 41), the 1588 Bible (p. 49), *Gwaedd Ynghymru* (p. 52), William Williams Pantycelyn (p. 65), the 1865 National Eisteddfod, Aberystwyth (p. 73), Daniel Owen (p. 76), and the photograph of Lewis Valentine, Saunders Lewis and D. J. Williams (p. 95), by permission of the National Library of Wales.

Lewis Morris (p. 60) and Caradoc Evans (p. 90) by permission of the National Museum of Wales.

T. H. Parry-Williams (p. 86), Gwyn Thomas (p. 103), Kate Roberts (p. 108), Dylan Thomas (p. 111), R. S. Thomas (p. 123), Emyr Humphreys (p. 125), Alan Llwyd (p. 129), and Gillian Clarke (p. 134), by permission of the Arts Council of Wales.

Idris Davies (p. 105) by permission of Gwyn and Ceinfryn Morris.

Poetry and prose extracts

'Death Song for Owain ab Urien', 'In Praise of Tenby', 'Sadness in Springtime', 'A Selection of Stanzas for the Harp', 'Song to the Nightingale', 'What Passes and Endures', an extract from 'The Departure of Arthur', (translations) from *Welsh Verse* (Seren Books, 1986) by permission of Anthony Conran.

'This Spot', 'J.S.L', an extract from 'In Berlin – August 1945', 'Preseli', 'A Little Monoglot Welsh Girl', translations by Joseph P. Clancy, from *Twentieth Century Welsh Poems* (1982) by permission of J. D. Lewis and Sons, Gwasg Gomer.

'I gaze across the distant hills' by William Williams, translated by H. Idris Bell, from *The Oxford Book of Welsh Verse in English*

(1977), reprinted from H. Idris Bell, *The Development of Welsh Poetry* (OUP, 1936), by permission of Oxford University Press.

'Blaen Cwrt', from Gillian Clarke, *Selected Poems* (1985), by permission of Carcanet Press.

'Gwalia Deserta XXVI', Idris Davies, by permission of Gwyn and Ceinfryn Morris.

'In Hospital: Poona (1)', Alun Lewis, by permission of Gweno Lewis.

'Reservoirs' by permission of R. S. Thomas.

'Tranc y Cof' by permission of Alan Llwyd.

'Israel', Harri Webb, by permission of Meic Stephens.

'Remembering Mari', Glyn Jones, by permission of Doreen Jones.

Extract from 'A Father in Sion', Caradoc Evans, from *My People* (1915, new edn. Seren, 1987) by permission of Seren Books.

Extracts from 'In Praise of Urien Rheged', translated by J. Saunders Lewis, and *Buchedd Garmon* by J. Saunders Lewis, by permission of Professor R. Geraint Gruffydd.

Extracts from *The Mabinogion* (1948) translated by Gwyn Jones and Thomas Jones, by permission of Professor Gwyn and Mrs Mair Jones.

Extracts from *Ellis Wynne* (Writers of Wales, 1984) by Gwyn Thomas and *Goronwy Owen* (Writers of Wales, 1986) by Branwen Jarvis, by permission of the University of Wales Press and the Arts Council of Wales.

Every effort has been made to trace the copyright holders of the extracts in this volume. In the case of any query, please contact the publishers.

1 Heroic Poetry

The poetic tradition

Two essential features of the Welsh poetic tradition are its antiquity and the continuity of its central theme of praise. By virtue of the works which have survived by two poets of the late sixth century, Taliesin and Aneirin, Welsh can claim to be the oldest attested vernacular literature in Europe. Welsh poets of the Middle Ages venerated Taliesin in particular as the founding father of the praise tradition, and deliberately wove echoes of the *hengerdd* (literally 'old song') into their own compositions. The elaborate patterning of sound which is a characteristic feature of the Welsh poetic craft is present in embryo in the earliest poetry. However, Taliesin and Aneirin should not in fact be seen as originators, but rather as inheritors of an already ancient and sophisticated bardic tradition common to the Celtic peoples and incorporating Indo-European social ideals. They stand at the very end of the Brythonic period of British history, nearly two hundred years after the end of the Roman occupation, and their work bears witness to the crucial conflict between the Brythonic tribes of northern Britain and the Germanic invaders.

The Old North

The earliest Welsh poetry is Welsh in a linguistic sense rather than a geographical one. In the late sixth century an early form of Welsh was spoken in the western half of Britain from southern Scotland down to Cornwall. Invading Germanic tribes occupied the eastern half of the island, and were gradually extending their territories westwards. Only one of Taliesin's surviving poems relates to the area now known as Wales. The rest of his work and all that of Aneirin belongs to the Brythonic kingdoms of what is now northern England and southern Scotland. The three independent kingdoms of that region were Rheged around the Solway estuary, Strathclyde further to the north around the estuary of the Clyde, and Gododdin to the east with its centre at Edinburgh. After the collapse of the kingdoms of Rheged and Gododdin in the seventh century, and the subsequent political isolation of Wales, the traditions and stories of the North may have been preserved in Strathclyde before being transmitted to Wales, where they came to represent the legendary heroic age of the Brythonic people, providing source material which Welsh poets and story-tellers were to draw on during the following centuries. There has been a good deal of scholarly debate over the authenticity of this early poetry, since the manuscript copies are of a much later date, and textual corruption no doubt occurred during the process of both oral and written transmission, but the general consensus is that a nucleus of genuine sixth-century material has survived in something close to its original form.

Taliesin

The work of Taliesin is preserved in a manuscript of the early fourteenth century known as the Book of Taliesin. Amongst that compendium of early and medieval poetry attributed to the legendary bard (see chapter 2), twelve poems have been distinguished as belonging to the late sixth century. Of these twelve, one is a panegyric addressed to Cynan Garwyn, a king of Powys in north-east Wales who flourished about the year 580, two are addressed to Gwallawg, the ruler of the small kingdom of Elmet (in the area around what is now Leeds), and the other nine all concern Urien, king of Rheged, and his son Owain. If all these poems are accepted as the genuine work of Taliesin, then it might be speculated that the poet was a native of Powys who migrated to the North, perhaps drawn by Urien's fame as a warlord. The existence of a poem of reconciliation (*dadolwch*) by Taliesin begging Urien's forgiveness may be connected to the two poems which he sang in praise of Urien's rival Gwallawg. However, it is equally possible that Taliesin was in fact a native of Rheged and Urien's court bard, and that the three poems to other lords were falsely attributed to him because of his legendary fame in a later period.

The essence of Taliesin's poetry is the depiction of the ideal ruler in the person of Urien Rheged, which can be seen to provide a model for the praise poetry of the next thousand years. The ideal is twofold, consisting of a balance between ferocity in leading his warriors to victory on the battlefield and magnanimous largesse towards his retainers in his court. The king is portrayed as personally responsible for the well-being of his people in war and in peace. Behind this ideal lies the primitive belief that the prosperity of a land depended on the kingly attributes of its ruler. The role of the poet's panegyric was to reassure the tribe that its ruler was indeed fit to be their king, proclaiming the righteousness of the established political order, whilst also serving to remind the king of his responsibilities towards his people.

Taliesin's poems are mostly short, averaging about thirty lines. His style is notable for its concision, achieved by taut phraseology and suggestive images. Even in his three poems celebrating Urien's martial exploits he does not provide any narrative account, but rather seeks to create a vivid impression of the events by striking visual details (such as dead warriors with light in their eyes, or the waters of a river like red wine with the blood of battle) and by dramatization. In 'The Battle of Argoed Llwyfain' we are given the very words of the enemy demanding hostages and the defiant replies of Owain and his father Urien. The ensuing slaughter is conveyed only by the image of ravens feeding on the corpses. The compressed intensity of the style is heightened by complex patterns of alliteration and internal rhyme, a feature which was later to develop into the formal system of *cynghanedd*. Key words can be effectively linked by consonantal correspondence, as in this laconic description of the aftermath of battle: 'A gwedy *bore*gat *bri*wgic' (And after morning battle hacked flesh).

One of the court poet's principal functions was the composition of an elegy (*marwnad*) on the death of his lord. Taliesin's elegy for Urien's son Owain is the earliest example of this important genre of Welsh poetry. It is more a celebration of his life than a lament on his death, declaring his superiority over his enemies with ferocious

Taliesin

'Death Song for Owain ab Urien'

God, consider the soul's need
    Of Owain son of Urien!
Rheged's prince, secret in loam:
    No shallow work, to praise him!

A strait grave, a man much praised,
    His whetted spear the wings of dawn:
That lord of bright Llwyfenydd,
    Where is his peer?

Reaper of enemies; strong of grip;
    One kind with his fathers;
Owain, to slay Fflamddwyn,
    Thought it no more than sleep.

Sleepeth the wide host of England
    With light in their eyes,
And those that had not fled
    Were braver than were wise.

Owain dealt them doom
    As the wolves devour sheep;
That warrior, bright of harness,
    Gave stallions for the bard.

Though he hoarded wealth like a miser,
    For his soul's sake he gave it.
God, consider the soul's need
    Of Owain son of Urien.

(Translation by Tony Conran, *Welsh Verse*)

relish. The prayer for the soul at the beginning and end of the poem shows that the poet was a Christian, but in proclaiming the undying fame of the warrior he was subscribing to a heroic ethic which was fundamentally pagan.

Aneirin

Roughly contemporary with Taliesin in the late sixth century, Aneirin was the author of a long poem known as the *Gododdin*, commemorating the heroic deeds of a war-band from the Gododdin tribe and their allies which was defeated by a much larger force from the Anglian kingdoms of Deira and Bernicia at the battle of Catraeth (probably Catterick in North Yorkshire) about the year 600. The battle is not attested in any other source, and the poem provides no narrative account, but the bare outlines of the event can be deduced. It seems that Mynyddawg Mwynfawr, lord of the Gododdin tribe, gathered together a select band of three hundred horsemen from all parts of the Brythonic world, who were feasted and trained for a year at his court of Dineidyn (Edinburgh) in preparation for an expedition against Catraeth, some one hundred and fifty miles to the south (probably accompanied by foot-soldiers). All except one were killed, but not before they had slain many times their own number of the enemy. The raid no doubt had some strategic purpose, but for Aneirin the most important thing was the warriors' loyalty to their lord. The heroic ethic demanded that in return for their lord's hospitality, symbolized by the mead which they drank in his hall, the warriors must be prepared to fight to the death for him on the battlefield. Honourable death in battle was the ultimate glory for the warriors, and the poet had a vital role to play in ensuring their everlasting fame.

The *Gododdin* is preserved in the Book of Aneirin, written in about 1265. The text consists of two independent versions, known as A and B, of which B has the more archaic orthography, probably deriving from an exemplar written in the ninth or tenth century. The substantial differences between the two texts suggest that the poem was transmitted orally before that. It is quite loose in form, consisting of about a thousand separate lines arranged in short rhyming stanzas. Each stanza is a separate unit, devoted either to one or several warriors, or to the war-band as a whole. Each encapsulates the whole sequence of events, involving a constantly shifting perspective, from the feasting beforehand, through the journey to Catraeth and the battle itself, to its aftermath of silence. Thus the poem as a whole is constantly circling around the central

A page from the Book of Aneirin.

event of the battle, having no linear development, no beginning or end.

Like Taliesin, Aneirin had a remarkable ability to epitomize the tragedy in one stark phrase, such as the second line of the first quotation given here, where the bitter irony is underlined by the

Aneirin

Three stanzas from the 'Gododdin'

Men went to Catraeth, swift was their host,
Fresh mead was their feast and it was poison,
Three hundred fighting according to plan,
And after jubilation there was silence.
Though they went to churches to do penance,
The inescapable meeting with death came to them.

* * *

The eminent Isag from the region of the South,
His manners were like the sea-flood
    For modesty and liberality
    And gracious mead-drinking.
Where his weapons struck there was no return blow,
He was unwavering in his ferocity.
His sword resounded in the heads of mothers,
Wall of battle, he was renowned, the son of Gwyddnau.

* * *

Bold in battle, resolute when hard-pressed,
In conflict he would make no truce,
In the day of wrath he would not shirk the fray.
Bleiddig son of Eli had the fury of a wild boar;
He drank wine from brimming glass vessels,
And performed great feats in the day of battle
Riding a white steed, before he died.
He left behind him bloodstained corpses.

rhyme between the words meaning feast and poison (*ancwyn* / *gwenwyn*). His awareness of the grief caused by his hero's action in the second quotation should not lead us to think that he felt pity for the bereaved mothers of his enemies. But, nevertheless, his clear-sighted recognition of the consequences of adherence to the heroic code meant that his exuberant praise of the warriors' prowess constantly gives way to grief at their deaths. It is from the tension between the conflicting moods of celebration and lament that the *Gododdin* derives much of its power.

Taliesin and Aneirin complement each other perfectly, one the poet of the warrior-king and the other of his faithful war-band. And yet in terms of their significance in the Welsh tradition they are diametrically opposed. Whereas Taliesin provided a model of the successful ruler, Aneirin celebrated heroic defeat. In view of the political history of the Welsh people, which has been one of resistance and loss since the early Middle Ages, it is not surprising that Aneirin's *Gododdin* should have particular resonance for them. And with the modern awareness of the tragic futility of war his poem has gained a new significance and provided inspiration for a number of poems about war, most notably David Jones's *In Parenthesis*.

Later heroic poetry

In contrast to the relative wealth of poetry from the end of the sixth century, the praise tradition is very sparsely represented over the following five centuries. There can be no doubt, however, that poetry did continue to be composed in the tradition of Taliesin and Aneirin, in praise of the rulers of the numerous independent kingdoms of Wales, but it has mostly not been preserved, either because it was never written down or because manuscripts have been lost. Isolated survivals from the seventh century which support such a belief are a stanza on the battle of Strathcarron (in 642) inserted into the text of the *Gododdin* at some later date, a poem in praise of Cadwallon ap Cadfan, king of Gwynedd, who defeated Edwin of Northumbria in 633, and an elegy for Cynddylan, king of Powys. Nothing has survived which can be definitely dated to the eighth century. The ninth century was very much the age of the saga poetry discussed in the next chapter. An outstanding poem from the end of that century which shows the continuity of the Taliesin tradition is 'Edmyg Dinbych' in praise of the royal court of Dyfed at Tenby, with its tantalizing reference to 'the writings of Britain'. The polemical spirit of the heroic age is seen in the rousing vaticinatory poem, 'Armes Prydein' ('The Prophecy of Britain'). Composed in south Wales in response to the attempt by Athelstan of Wessex to exact tributes from the Welsh princes in the 930s, the prophecy foretells a Celtic alliance of forces from Wales, Cornwall, Brittany, Ireland and the Old North which will drive the English out of the island of Britain.

A ninth-century poem by an unknown writer
from 'Praise of Tenby'

There is a fine fortress of revel and tumult
A multitude makes, and crying of birds.
Gay was that company met at the Calends
Round a generous lord, splendid and brave.
Before he had gone to the oaken church
From a bowl of glass gave me mead and wine.

There is a fine fortress on the foreshore,
Finely to each is given his share.
I know at Tenby – pure white the seagull –
Companions of Bleiddud, lord of the court.
The night of the Calends it was my custom
To lie by my king, brilliant in war,
With a cloak coloured purple, having such cheer
I were the tongue to the poets of Britain!

There is a fine fortress resounds with song,
Where every concession I wished for was mine –
I say nothing of rights! I kept good order:
Whoever knows otherwise deserves no feast-gift!
The writings of Britain were my chief care
Where the loud waves broke in tumult.
Let it long remain, that cell I visited!

(Translation by Tony Conran, *Welsh Verse*)

2 Early Medieval Poetry

Saga poetry

Unlike the heroic poetry discussed in the previous chapter, saga poems are not a direct response to the events of history, but imaginative compositions based on legends about the past. Most of the saga poems were composed in the ninth and tenth centuries by a number of different authors working in the same tradition, all anonymous. They refer to characters and events of the sixth and seventh centuries, in the context of warfare with the Anglo-Saxons either in the Old North or on the border between Wales and England. The poems do not narrate the events on which they are based, but are dramatic utterances by the characters. It used to be thought that they formed part of a recitation of the whole story in prose, verse being used to mark the emotional high points, and that only the verse parts had a fixed form to be committed to writing. However, there is no firm evidence to support such a theory, and it is equally possible that these poems would have been performed independently, referring to stories well known to the original audiences. There are three main cycles, that is groups of poems relating to the same story material. The most obscure is that which relates to the death of Urien Rheged (Taliesin's patron). In the main poem of the cycle the unidentified speaker is carrying off Urien's head from the battlefield, and at the same time lamenting his death. The other two cycles are much clearer, with very strongly characterized main speakers, Llywarch Hen and Heledd.

The englyn metre

Most of the saga poems are composed in the three-line *englyn* metre, of which there are two main types, the simple *englyn milwr* with three monorhymed lines of equal length, and the more complex *englyn penfyr* with lengthened first line and short second. The set stanzaic structure is very effective for dramatic exchanges between characters and also in conveying intense emotion through incremental repetition of key phrases. The ornamentation of the *englynion* sequences is just as elaborate as that of the praise poetry, and there is no reason to suppose that their authors were of lower status than the court poets of the period. The earliest recorded

10

examples of Welsh poetry are in the *englyn* metre, a religious piece and a fragment of a lost saga poem, known as the Juvencus *englynion* from the contents of the Latin manuscript in which they were written in the late ninth or early tenth century. The *englyn* metre was used quite extensively for gnomic or proverbial statement based on descriptions of the natural world, which is also a feature of some of the saga poetry.

The Llywarch Hen cycle

Llywarch Hen ('the old') is known from genealogical tracts as a cousin of Urien Rheged, which provides a tenuous link between two of the cycles. However, he has been transferred from his northern British background and relocated in Wales in the context of border conflict with the English (perhaps originally associated with the royal and monastic site at Llan-gors near Brecon). As his epithet suggests, he is consistently portrayed as an old man, and his story centres on his relationship with his twenty-four sons. He is seen in dialogue poems urging them to extremes of heroism, with the result that all are killed and Llywarch is left to lament them and blame himself for their deaths. Considerable dramatic tension is generated in his exchange with the last of his sons, Gwên, whom he taunts with the accusation of cowardice. Llywarch's boast of his own former prowess is met by Gwên's sarcastic comment, 'You are alive and your witness slain. No old man was a weakling in his youth.' Nevertheless, Gwên goes to stand guard at the ford, and is duly killed. In recognizing that it was his tongue which brought about his sons' deaths, Llywarch comes close to casting doubt on the heroic ideal of death in battle as the warrior's highest honour. Bravery is still an admirable quality, but the simple values of the heroic age are here seen from a different perspective from that of the praise poet. The emphasis in the saga poetry is less on the deeds of the dead hero than on the psychological state of the lone survivor, and the self-knowledge which derives from his or her suffering (for which parallels can be found in Old English and Irish poetry of the same period). The Llywarch Hen cycle comes to a powerful climax with the old man's moving lament for all that he has lost, which has both dramatic force and universality.

The Heledd cycle

The central event of this cycle is the death of Cynddylan, a king of northern Powys in the seventh century (to whom a genuine elegy

The Llywarch Hen Cycle
from 'The Old Man's Lament'

Old age is mocking me
From my hair to my teeth
And the knob women used to love.

Swirling the wind. White the skirts
Of the trees. The stag is bold, the hill bleak.
Frail is the old man; slowly he rises.

This leaf, driven here and there by the wind,
Woe to it for its fate.
It is old. This year it was born.

What I loved as a youth is hateful to me:
A girl, a stranger, and an unbroken horse.
No indeed, they do not suit me.

* * *

Neither sleep nor merriment comes to me
Since Llawr and Gwên were killed.
I am a cantankerous carcass – I am old.

Wretched the fortune assigned to Llywarch
From the night he was born:
Long hardship and never-ending weariness.

from that period has survived), and the devastation of his territory by the English of Mercia. However, the poems should not be taken as an accurate representation of the history of seventh-century Powys, since Cynddylan may actually have been in alliance with Mercia. They most probably reflect the background of border conflict in the period of their composition in the ninth century. Cynddylan is lamented by his sister Heledd, whose role is similar to that of Llywarch Hen as the lone survivor suffering the consequences of warfare. But Heledd is a more passive figure than

Llywarch, and this cycle has a greater lyric intensity in its focus on her grief (perhaps reflecting women's function as keeners in funeral rites). The obsessional quality of her grief, bordering on insanity, is powerfully conveyed by the technique of incremental repetition in sequences meditating on his ruined hall, on the ravaged townships of his territory, and, most painful of all, on the eagles which will feed on his flesh. At the heart of the cycle is Heledd's stark evocation of loss and desolation in the famous sequence about his hall, 'Stafell Gynddylan'. Together with a similar piece about the ruined court of Rheged in the Urien cycle, this is the beginning of a long tradition of Welsh poems which have particular resonance in modern times as images of social disintegration.

The Heledd Cycle
from 'Cynddylan's Hall'

Dark is Cynddylan's hall tonight,
    With no fire, no bed.
  I will weep awhile, then I will fall silent.

Dark is Cynddylan's hall tonight,
    With no fire, no candle.
  Save for God, who will give me sanity?

Dark is Cynddylan's hall tonight,
    With no fire, no light.
  Grief for you overcomes me.

It pierces me to see Cynddylan's hall
    With no roof, no fire.
  Dead is my lord; I myself alive.

Desolate is Cynddylan's hall tonight
    After staunch warriors,
  Elfan and gold-adorned Cynddylan.

Cold and bare is Cynddylan's hall tonight
    After the respect I had,
  Without the men and the women who maintained it.

Other saga poems

Some poems of this type probably involve no more than a dramatized situation without a full story behind it, such as the passionate complaint of the Leper of Abercuawg, a striking use of nature description in bitter contrast to the speaker's emotional state. Others seem to be fragments to which the narrative key is now lost. The most tantalizing of these are the poems relating to King Arthur, relics of what seems to have been a rich body of Welsh traditions about him predating Geoffrey of Monmouth. In a poem known from its first line as 'Pa gur yw y porthaur' ('What man is the gatekeeper?') Arthur is seen with his band of followers seeking entrance to a fortress. Arthur appears in a mythological context in the poem 'Preiddiau Annwfn', an account of his expedition in his ship *Prydwen* to capture a magic cauldron from the Celtic Otherworld, depicted as a glass fortress on an island. The popular belief that Arthur was still alive, and would one day return to lead

The nature convention and elegiac mood are used with moving effect in an anonymous religious poem found in the Black Book of Carmarthen, probably a product of the monastic revival of the twelfth century.

'Sadness in Springtime'

Month of May, loveliest season,
The birds loud, the growth green,
Plough in furrow, ox in yoke,
Green sea, land cut dapple.

In the fine treetops when cuckoos sing,
    My sadness is greater:
    Smoke smart, manifest sleep-lack
    For my kinsfolk gone to rest.

In hill, in dale, in isles of the sea,
    Wheresoever one may go,
    From blest Christ there's no escaping.

(Translated by Tony Conran, *Welsh Verse*)

auty tawian · hid attad y
daeth rad kyulaun · llat
kyndur tra messury ku
ynan · llas haelon odin
on tra uuan ꞏ Thy uir ·
nod maur eu clod · gan ·
elgan · Mirdh · Thuy a th
tui · Ruy · a Ruy · trav ath
tau undoech y doethan ·

A page from the Black Book of Carmarthen (Folio 2).

his people to victory, is seen in one of the *Englynion y Beddau* ('Stanzas of the Graves'), where it is stated that his grave will not be found until the Judgement Day.

The poet as seer

The image of the poet as sober craftsman and upholder of the social order has predominated in the Welsh poetic tradition, exemplified by the historical Taliesin, but a very different image has always had a strong hold on the popular imagination, that of the wild inspired seer, for which the archetype is found in legends about Taliesin and Myrddin. As a result of his high bardic status the figure of Taliesin became associated with a folk tale concerning the origin of poetic inspiration, known as *Hanes Taliesin*, which probably evolved in the ninth or tenth century (although the earliest recorded version dates from the sixteenth century). After accidentally swallowing three drops from the magic cauldron of the witch Ceridwen, Gwion Bach goes through a series of transformations before being reincarnated as the poet Taliesin, imbued with the gift of prophecy. Taliesin's shamanistic persona is very prominent in the poems attributed to him in the Book of Taliesin, where he is presented as the possessor of arcane knowledge (including a good deal of Christian learning). Unlike Taliesin, Myrddin seems to have been purely a figure of legend, having affinities with the Irish Suibhne Geilt. He was held to have received the gift of prophecy as a result of a terrifying vision which he saw during the battle of Arfderydd (believed to have been fought in the Old North in 573), after which he lived as a wild man in Celyddon Wood. He is not to be confused with the Arthurian wizard Myrddin (Merlin), who was an invention of Geoffrey of Monmouth in the twelfth century. The figures of Taliesin and Myrddin were used in the Middle Ages to give authority to numerous obscure vaticinatory poems prophesying victory over the Saxons.

3 Medieval Prose

The story-teller

The medieval Welsh story-teller was known as *y cyfarwydd* (literally 'the learned one'), a term which indicates that he was expected to possess a wealth of traditional stories and lore (*cyfarwyddyd*). Like the poets, he would have had high social status as a court entertainer. His art was essentially an oral one, requiring a powerful memory and a ready command of story-telling techniques and formulae in order to recreate stories at each performance. Although the tradition of oral story-telling continued into the modern period, very little has been preserved (in contrast to the abundance of stories surviving from early Ireland), and the few prose tales which do exist in medieval manuscripts are deliberate literary compositions by individual authors who were familiar with the art of the *cyfarwydd*. However, the vast extent of the Welsh story-teller's repertoire is evident from surviving fragments and allusions to lost tales, such as the Triads (characters and episodes arranged in groups of three as a mnemonic device), the lists of heroes' burial places known as *Englynion y Beddau* ('Stanzas of the Graves)', and many passing references in medieval poetry.

The Mabinogion

The term *Mabinogi* seems to have originally meant 'boyhood', and then 'a tale of a hero's boyhood', and eventually 'a tale' in general. The plural form *Mabinogion* is in fact a ghost-word occurring due to scribal error at the end of the first of the Four Branches of the Mabinogi, but it was adopted by Charlotte Guest as the title of her collection of translations of the medieval tales made between 1838 and 1849. It has become established as a convenient term for the whole group of eleven tales, *Mabinogi* being reserved for the Four Branches only. The texts are preserved in two important compendia of medieval Welsh literature, the White Book of Rhydderch, written about the middle of the fourteenth century, and the slightly later Red Book of Hergest (fragments of the Four Branches also occur in MS Peniarth 6 of *c.* 1225–35). One typical feature of the oral tradition which has clung to these tales is that all are anonymous.

The Four Branches of the Mabinogi

The *Mabinogi* consists of four distinct tales which are rather tenuously linked to one another. Each concludes with the formula: 'Thus ends this branch (*cainc*) of the *Mabinogi*.' Whether they originally formed an organic whole has been a matter of considerable debate. The only character who occurs in all four branches is Pryderi, who is born in the first and killed in the last, and it has been argued that the *Mabinogi* originally told his life story. However, such a scheme is hardly evident in the tales as they stand, and recent criticism has tended to focus more on the qualities of the work as a deliberate literary composition. Evenness of style and tone suggests that the four are the work of a single author, who may well have been a cleric, probably in the latter half of the eleventh century. Some of his material undoubtedly derived from a much earlier period, originally involving mythological figures such as the giant Brân or Bendigeidfran fab Llŷr, the prototype of Bron the Fisher King in the Grail legend, and Lleu, who corresponds to the Celtic god Lugus (from whom the cities of Lyons, Laon, and Leyden derive their names). International popular motifs such as 'The Calumniated Wife' (which occurs in the first and second branches) and 'The Forbidden Door' are another prominent element in the make-up of the tales. In terms of plot the author's contribution was probably that of redactor, arranging and rationalizing inherited material, with varying degrees of success. Some inconsistencies remain, but on the whole the stories are told extremely effectively, with a purposeful narrative style and vivid characterization, in which succinctly revealing dialogue plays a major part. There is little authorial intervention in the tales, and no attempt to moralize about the marvellous and often tragic events related, but nevertheless recurrent themes can be discerned, and the work can be seen to project a consistent attitude towards life, upholding reasonable and moderate conduct, an ideal embodied not least by the clarity and restraint of the author's style.

The first branch consists of three distinct episodes in the life of the hero, Pwyll, lord of Dyfed in south-west Wales. In the first he changes places with the king of Annwfn (the Otherworld) for a year, as a result of which he gains the title 'Head of Annwfn'. The second episode is his marriage to Rhiannon, and the third is the birth and mysterious disappearance of their son Pryderi, who is eventually restored to them, releasing Rhiannon from her penance for having killed him. Pwyll comes across as a dependable but rather slow-witted character, in contrast to the shrewd and resourceful

Rhiannon. For instance, when a visitor to the wedding feast requests a boon, Pwyll foolishly promises to give him anything he wants, and is dumbfounded when he demands Rhiannon. Her cutting comment is a nice example of the succinct use of dialogue to reveal character: '"Be dumb as long as thou wilt," said Rhiannon. "Never was there a man made feebler use of his wits than thou hast."' She then proceeds to devise a trick to enable Pwyll to win her back.

The second branch has the most satisfying narrative structure, with a very tight sequence of cause and effect, and it is also the most emotionally intense of the four, a savagely realistic story illumined by moments of pathos and lyricism. Its central theme can be seen as the terrible destructive force of jealousy and the desire for vengeance. The principal characters are the children of Llŷr, the giant Brân, king of Britain, his sister Branwen, and their half-brother, the troublemaker Efnisien. Branwen is married to Matholwch, king of Ireland, at Brân's court at Harlech, but Efnisien is angry that he was not consulted, and retaliates by mutilating Matholwch's horses. Matholwch is duly recompensed and returns home with his bride, but the people of Ireland are not satisfied, and persuade the king to punish Branwen. She manages to send a bird over the sea with a message to her brother, who comes to her rescue. The conflict is about to be settled peacefully when Efnisien again stirs up strife by the breathtakingly savage act of hurling Branwen's infant son into the fire. In the ensuing slaughter Ireland is almost entirely depopulated, and only seven men survive to bring Brân's severed head back to Wales, where Branwen dies of a broken heart at having been the cause of so much destruction. The survivors are solaced by the magic song of the birds of Rhiannon, and by a timeless feast on the island of Gwales, until the spell is broken and they must go to bury Brân's head in the White Hill in London.

The third branch follows on from the second, and also has links with the first. Brân's brother Manawydan, one of the survivors of the expedition to Ireland, is befriended by Pryderi and marries his mother, the widowed Rhiannon. Dyfed is laid waste by an enchantment, which turns out to be the work of a magician in revenge for the ill-treatment of Rhiannon's suitor by Pwyll in the first branch. Manawydan and Pryderi go to work in England as humble craftsmen, and on their return Pryderi and Rhiannon are imprisoned in a magic fortress. Manawydan finally succeeds in lifting the enchantment by threatening to hang a mouse caught

The Second Branch of the Mabinogi

Efnisien throws Branwen's son into the fire

And with that the hosts came into the house. And the men of the Island of Ireland came into the house on the one side, and the men of the Island of the Mighty on the other. And as soon as they were seated there was concord between them, and the kingship was conferred upon the boy. And then, when peace was concluded, Bendigeidfran called the boy to him. From Bendigeidfran the boy went to Manawydan, with all who saw him loving him. From Manawydan, Nisien son of Euroswydd called the boy to him. The boy went to him in friendship. 'Why,' said Efnisien, 'comes not my nephew, my sister's son, to me? Though he were not king of Ireland, gladly would I show love to the boy.' 'Let him go, gladly,' said Bendigeidfran. The boy went to him gladly. 'By my confession to God,' said Efnisien in his heart, 'an enormity the household would not think might be committed is the enormity I shall now commit.' And he arose and took up the boy by the feet and made no delay, nor did a man in the house lay hold on him before he thrust the boy headlong into the blazing fire. And when Branwen saw her son burning in the fire, she made as if to leap into the fire from the place where she was sitting between her two brothers. And Bendigeidfran grasped her with one hand, and his shield with the other. And then they all rose up throughout the house; and that was the greatest tumult that was by a host in one house, as each man caught up arms ... And while each man reached for his arms, Bendigeidfran supported Branwen between his shield and his shoulder.

(Translation from Gwyn Jones and Thomas Jones, *The Mabinogion*)

devouring his corn, which is actually the magician's wife. Manawydan's patience and resourcefulness in the face of adversity can be seen to represent the author's view of the ideal human qualities, although it is debatable whether the original story was intended to present him in such a positive light.

The last and most complex of the Four Branches concerns the family of Dôn in north Wales. Math, king of Gwynedd, can only live with his feet in a maiden's lap, except when he is waging war. Gilfaethwy fab Dôn falls in love with Math's foot-bearer, and in order to give him a chance to rape her his brother Gwydion brings about war between Gwynedd and the southern kingdom of Deheubarth, which incidentally results in Pryderi's death. Math then needs a new foot-bearer, and Gwydion's sister Aranrhod applies for the post, but fails the virginity test. She gives birth to a son who is brought up by Gwydion. When confronted with the boy Aranrhod swears that he will have no name unless she gives him one. Gwydion tricks her by his magic into calling him Lleu Llawgyffes ('the fair one with the deft hand'), upon which she swears he will never bear arms unless she gives him them. When Gwydion tricks her into arming him she condemns him never to have a mortal wife. Gwydion and Math create a woman out of flowers for him, called Blodeuwedd ('Flower Face'), but she turns out to be a disastrous wife, taking a lover and helping him to murder Lleu. Gwydion restores Lleu to life by his magic and punishes Blodeuwedd by turning her into an owl. The havoc wreaked by uncontrolled sexual desire is a notable theme in this branch, and the role played by the magician Gwydion is an ambiguous one, both destructive in bringing about the unnecessary death of Pryderi to consummate his brother's lust, and constructive in his care for Lleu to counteract his sister's malice.

The Four Branches is arguably Wales's greatest contribution to European literature, and of all the Welsh classics it is certainly the one which loses least in translation. In addition to the appeal of well-told and moving stories, several of the characters and motifs have captured the modern imagination and stimulated authors in both Welsh and English. The enchantment on Dyfed has been a resonant image of language loss, the birds of Rhiannon have been used by several poets to represent the healing power of art, and above all the enigmatic figure of Blodeuwedd has been a fascinating subject, most notably in the drama by Saunders Lewis discussed in chapter 9.

Arthurian tales

The crucial dividing line in Arthurian literature is Geoffrey of Monmouth's *Historia Regum Britanniae* of *c.* 1138. Although

Geoffrey certainly drew on some Welsh traditions about Arthur, his portrait of the emperor presiding over a chivalric court was a new contribution which laid the basis for a vast European literature of Arthurian romance. Three of the Welsh Arthurian tales belong to that romance genre, but *Culhwch and Olwen* pre-dates Geoffrey, and the later *Dream of Rhonabwy* is also in the native tradition.

Culhwch and Olwen is the earliest extant Arthurian tale in any language, belonging in its surviving redaction to the second half of the eleventh century. Arthur's role as leader of a band of warriors is already established, but he is a rougher and more actively heroic figure than in the later romances. Culhwch is fated by his stepmother to marry none other than Olwen, daughter of the giant Ysbaddaden, and he enlists the help of his cousin Arthur to fulfil the seemingly impossible tasks set as conditions by her father. This well-known tale-type serves as the framework for a number of independent stories, such as the boisterous hunting of the monstrous boar Twrch Trwyth. The style of the tale is extravagantly hyperbolical, studded with rhetorical set pieces, and reflects an aspect of the oral story-teller's craft which is in complete contrast to the restraint of the Four Branches. The action is often farcical, and gives the impression of being a burlesque of the traditional hero tales.

The Dream of Rhonabwy is an enigmatic satirical work which has given rise to varying interpretations. The framework of the dream is set in Powys during the reign of Madog ap Maredudd, who died in 1160, but the tale is not necessarily contemporary with its setting, and could well have been written in the thirteenth century. The dream vision which Rhonabwy experiences as a result of sleeping on a yellow ox skin is set in a legendary Arthurian past, and part of the satirical intent is to belittle contemporary society by comparison with figures from the heroic age. Arthur smiles on seeing that 'men as mean as these keep this island, after men as fine as those that kept it of yore'. But there is nothing heroic about the portrait of Arthur and his fellows, and the satire seems to be directed equally against the myths of the heroic past. This is the most consciously literary of the medieval Welsh prose tales, attacking court bards for the obscurity of their praise poetry, and even perhaps parodying the inconsequential narratives of Arthurian romance.

The three romances

The three Arthurian romances, *Owain* (or *The Lady of the Fountain*), *Geraint and Enid*, and *Peredur*, correspond quite closely to works by the twelfth-century French poet Chrétien de Troyes, *Yvain, Erec et Enide*, and *Perceval*. The relationship between the Welsh and French texts is still a matter for debate, but it seems likely that their common sources were Welsh. Chivalric elements in the Welsh tales derived from the Norman culture which was well established in south Wales by the second half of the twelfth century, providing a channel for contacts between Wales and the Continent. In style and story-telling technique the romances are quite similar to the *Four Branches*, but the focus on the character of the individual knight-errant gives them an entirely different quality. The Welsh authors show much less interest in the theory of chivalry than does Chrétien, preferring to maintain a swift narrative pace, but nevertheless the very structure of the tales highlights the moral development of the hero.

Peredur deals with the chivalric education of a lad of noble birth whose mother has kept him in ignorance of the knightly way of life for his own safety. The process is essentially one of drawing out his innate knighthood, beginning with his arrival at Arthur's court, where he learns to devote his strength to the defence of the weak, and culminating in his experience of love as the deepest motivation for his valour. The structure of the tale is diffuse, and becomes confused towards the end, including a perfunctory treatment of the Grail theme, but its strength lies in the sympathetic portrayal of the young hero.

The central theme of both *Owain* and *Geraint and Enid* is the problem of the relationship between love and martial prowess in the chivalric ideal, with the respective heroes going to opposite extremes. Owain kills the Lord of the Fountain in combat, and eventually marries his widow, but then neglects her by returning to Arthur's court. Geraint, on the other hand, becomes obsessed with his young wife Enid and neglects his duties as a knight. In both cases the ideal balance is only restored after a period of penance and self-imposed hardship. *Owain* in particular is a sophisticated work of literature using subtle characterization and a carefully organized narrative structure to exemplify the tension inherent in the ideals of its society.

Owain

Owain sees the Lady of the Fountain mourning her husband

And Owain arose and dressed himself and opened a chamber window and looked towards the city, and he saw neither limit nor bound to the hosts filling the streets, and they fully armed, and many ladies with them horsed and a-foot, and all the clerics of the city chanting. And it seemed to Owain that the air rang, so great was the outcry and the trumpets and the clerics chanting. And in the middle of that host he could see the bier, and a pall of white bliant thereon, and wax tapers burning in great numbers around it, and there was not one man carrying the bier of lower rank than a mighty baron.

And Owain was certain he had never beheld a train so beautiful as that with brocaded silk and satin and sendal. And following that host he could see a yellow-haired lady with her hair over her shoulders, and many a gout of blood on her tresses, and a torn garment of yellow brocaded silk about her, and two buskins of speckled cordwain upon her feet. And it was a marvel that the ends of her fingers were not maimed, so hard did she beat her two hands together. And Owain was certain that he had never beheld a lady as lovely as she, were she in her right guise. And louder was her shrieking than what there was of man and horn in the host. And when he beheld the lady he was fired with love of her, till each part of him was filled therewith. And Owain asked the maiden who the lady was. 'God knows,' said the maiden, 'a lady of whom it may be said that she is the fairest of women, and the most chaste, and the most generous, and the wisest and noblest. My mistress is she, and the Lady of the Fountain she called, wife to the man thou slewest yesterday.' 'God knows of me,' said Owain, 'she is the lady I love best.' 'God knows,' said the maiden, 'she loves not thee, neither a little nor at all.'

Translation from Gwyn Jones and Thomas Jones, *The Mabinogion*)

Pseudo-historical tales

Of the two tales dealing with traditions about early British history, the shortest and plainest is *Lludd and Llefelys*, of which the earliest version was inserted into a Welsh translation of the *Historia Regum Britanniae* in about 1200. According to Geoffrey, Lludd was king of Britain shortly before Julius Caesar's invasion, and in this story he enlists the help of his brother Llefelys, king of France, to ward off three supernatural oppressions from the island (probably a popular reworking of the theme of defence against foreign invaders). *The Dream of Macsen Wledig* is a much more satisfying tale, probably dating from the twelfth century, in which pseudo-historical traditions are combined with folk-tale motifs. The hero is based on the Magnus Maximus of history who was proclaimed emperor of Rome by his troops in Britain in AD 383. In the tale he is already emperor when he comes to Wales from Rome to seek out a beautiful maiden he has seen in a dream vision, the legendary Elen of the Hosts, and then has to return with Elen's brothers to regain his throne which has been usurped in his absence. The tale explains the Brythonic emigration to Brittany by having Macsen grant land there to Elen's brother Cynan Meiriadog.

Translations

By the later Middle Ages the native prose tradition seems to have been in decline, and most of the works commissioned by the Welsh nobility from the late thirteenth century onwards were translations of popular European tales, especially from the French. The translations follow the medieval practice of free adaptation according to native literary and cultural conventions, using the narrative style familiar from the native tales. The Arthurian romances were supplemented by *Ystoryaeu y Seint Greal*, a lengthy translation of two independent French texts concerning the search for the Grail. A less high-minded tale of martial exploits is the romance of Beves of Hampton, translated into Welsh from a lost Anglo-Norman poem. But most popular of all were the *chansons de geste* of Charlemagne and his knights, presenting a more primitive warrior ideal which accorded well with the Welsh heroic tradition. A series of separate texts were translated into Welsh to form a cycle known as *Ystorya de Carolo Magno*.

Functional prose

Creative and functional writing were not rigidly distinguished in the Middle Ages, and a number of other genres must be taken into account in order to appreciate the full scope of medieval Welsh prose literature. The range of fields covered included history, law,

This illustration from the Welsh Laws in MS Peniarth 28 probably depicts the servant and maidservant of the chamber.

geography, medicine, hagiography and theology. Most of these were translations from Latin texts, with a few from French and English. Several collections of religious prose have survived, the most important being the Book of the Anchorite of 1346, which includes basic texts necessary for the priest to instruct his parishioners in the vernacular, the lives of St David and St Beuno, a translation of a popular theological text, the *Elucidarium*, and an original mystical work entitled *Ymborth yr Enaid* ('Food for the Soul'). Historical writing was of vital importance to the Welsh sense of national identity, proclaiming their classical origin from Brutus of Troy and their right to the sovereignty of the whole island of Britain, and providing a foundation for the tradition of prophetic poetry. Three separate texts were linked to provide a full national history centring on the Welsh version of Geoffrey of Monmouth's story of the British golden age, *Brut y Brenhinedd*, which was prefaced by an account of the Trojan war translated from the Latin, and continued up to the loss of independence at the end of the thirteenth century by the annals of the Welsh princes, *Brut y Tywysogion.*

The oldest and most important category of functional prose in Welsh was the native law, known as the 'Law of Hywel Dda' after the tenth-century king who is supposed to have reorganized the laws of Wales. Some forty medieval law manuscripts have survived, written by professional lawyers from the twelfth century onwards. There were close links between law and literature in medieval Wales, and the depiction of social relationships in the laws frequently illuminates both the prose tales and the poetry. The precision and clarity of expression achieved in the law-books is the culmination of a long tradition of legal writing in Welsh, and can be seen to have laid the basis for the stylistic excellence of the *Mabinogion.*

From the Life of St David
The death of St David

On Sunday David sang a mass, and he preached a sermon to the people. And its like had never been heard before him, nor will it ever be heard after him. No one ever saw so many people in one place. And after finishing the sermon and the mass, David gave a general blessing to all who were there. And after he had given the blessing to everyone, he said these words, 'Lords, brothers and sisters, be joyful and keep your faith and your religion, and do the little things which you have heard and seen from me. And I will walk the way which our fathers went, and farewell to you,' said David. 'And may you be mighty on the earth, and we will never see each other again.' ... And on Tuesday eve about cock-crow, behold a host of angels filling the city, and all manner of songs and delight everywhere throughout the city. And at daybreak, behold the Lord Jesus Christ coming, and the nine orders of heaven with him, as he had departed in his majesty, and the brilliant sun illuminating all the hosts. And that was on Tuesday, the first day of the month of March, that Jesus Christ took the soul of St David with great triumph and joy and honour.

4 Medieval Poetry

The Poets of the Princes

After the scarcity of material from the early Middle Ages, the praise tradition is well attested again in the twelfth and thirteenth centuries. The impression of a sudden revival is no doubt an illusion created by the accidents of manuscript survival. The principal source for this poetry is the Hendregadredd manuscript, which has the appearance of being a deliberate collection made at the very end of the era of the independent Welsh princes around 1300, containing the finest works of the previous two centuries. Nevertheless, the high standards and exuberance of Welsh poetry in this period may well be related both to the general flourishing of European court culture in the twelfth century, and to the military successes of the Welsh princes against the Anglo-Normans at this time.

The Poets of the Princes are so called because of their close association with the royal families of the three independent kingdoms of Wales, Gwynedd in the north, Powys in mid-Wales, and Deheubarth in the south. They are also sometimes known as *y Gogynfeirdd* (literally 'the fairly early poets', as distinct from *y Cynfeirdd*, 'the early poets'), but that term can include poets who continued to compose in the same mode for about a century after the era of the independent princes. They had privileged status as court poets, with duties and rights defined by the law-codes, and formed a closely knit bardic order of trained professionals. The highest rank was that of *pencerdd* ('chief-of-song'), whose pre-eminence was indicated by a special chair in the royal court (the origin of the eisteddfodic practice of chairing the winning poet), where he was expected to sing two songs, one to God and the other to the king. The *bardd teulu* ('poet of the retinue') was one of the twenty-four officers of the court, whose duties involved singing to the war-band before battle and also singing to the queen in her private chamber. Lowest in rank were the *cerddorion* (Latin *joculatores*). It is not clear to what extent this classification reflected actual bardic practice in the twelfth century. The evidence of the surviving poetry suggests that the same poet could fulfil the roles of both *pencerdd* and *bardd teulu*, but the distinction between them is still significant in that it represents two different aspects of the poet's function, formal celebration and more informal entertainment.

The praise poetry of the court poets was composed in a highly ornate style, using much archaic diction and loose syntax based primarily on the juxtaposition of descriptive phrases. Great emphasis was placed on the ornamentation of sound, developing and formalizing the use of alliteration and rhyme already present in the earliest Welsh poetry. The poems were recited to the accompaniment of the harp (although nothing is known of the precise nature of that accompaniment), and the performance would have been an extremely impressive piece of court ceremony. The main poetic form used was the *awdl*, employing one or more of a number of intricate metres (later codified as a system of twenty-four, which has survived in use until the present day). The *awdl* was originally a relatively short monorhymed piece (the word is cognate with *odl*, 'rhyme'), but the *Gogynfeirdd* composed much longer poems with sections on different rhymes. They also composed sequences of four-line *englynion*, which may originally have been a less ceremonial form used by the *bardd teulu*.

The surviving corpus of court poetry from the twelfth and thirteenth centuries is the work of about thirty poets, although some are represented by only one poem. Almost half of it consists of the work of two major poets, Cynddelw Brydydd Mawr of Powys and Llywarch ap Llywelyn, the bard of Llywelyn the Great of Gwynedd. The earliest known poet of the period is Meilyr Brydydd, whose son Gwalchmai and grandsons Einion and Meilyr ap Gwalchmai are a good example of a bardic family. However, the bardic craft does not seem to have been hereditary in Wales to the extent that it was in medieval Ireland. There are two examples of amateur poets of royal blood, Hywel ab Owain Gwynedd, the outstanding love poet of the period, and Owain Cyfeiliog of Powys, whose 'Hirlas Owain' ('Owain's Drinking-horn') celebrated a successful expedition by his war-band in 1155.

Cynddelw Brydydd Mawr

Cynddelw's sobriquet ('the great poet') most likely referred originally to his physical size, but soon came to denote his pre-eminence amongst the poets of his period. Nearly four thousand lines of his work have survived, and he is the most representative of the Poets of the Princes. He seems to have been a native of Powys, and began his career towards the end of the reign of Madog ap

Cynddelw Brydydd Mawr

the opening lines of 'Elegy for Madog ap Maredudd'

I beseech my King to give me hope of grace,
I beseech, as I have done a hundred times,
To seek to fashion a bright song of my finest language
    To my lord and comrade,
To lament the grief of Madog the giver of mead-feasts,
    Whose enemies are in every land:
Door of a fortress, companion like a shield,
Buckler in the thrust of battle, in a fine fight,
The tumult of fire roaring through heather,
Scatterer of his foes, a shield in slaughter.
Chieftain celebrated in song, hope of minstrels,
Red, irresistible, unswerving comrade.

Maredudd in the 1150s. After Madog's death in 1160 he served the princes of the divided kingdom of Powys, but also sang to Owain Gwynedd and the Lord Rhys of Deheubarth, demonstrating the freedom enjoyed by the foremost poets to travel throughout Wales. His work covers all the topics and genres of medieval Welsh poetry, under the three main headings of praise, religion, and love. Eulogy and elegy make up the greater part of his work, of course, but he also sang poems of reconciliation (*dadolwch*), of thanks for gifts, and affirmed the rights of the freemen of his native Powys. One of his most moving compositions is an elegy on the death of his own son Dygynnelw, the earliest example of a genre which is quite well attested in Welsh in the later Middle Ages. His religious poetry includes two *awdlau* in praise of God, which may represent the *pencerdd*'s duty to sing first to God, one to St Tysilio exalting his shrine at Meifod in Powys, and a poem of death-bed repentance (*marwysgafn*), which seems to have been an established convention amongst the Poets of the Princes. One of his two love poems is addressed to an unnamed girl, and contains the earliest reference in Welsh to the stock figure of the jealous husband, suggesting a familiarity with the conventions of European love literature. The other is along and elaborate composition professing love for the princess Efa, daughter of Madog ap Maredudd, probably in fact a sophisticated form of praise. This also appears to reflect the

European fashion of courtly love, but it is unlikely that Troubadour influence could have reached Wales so soon, and this is probably an instance of similar social circumstances producing a similar attitude of devotion towards a noble patroness. Through all Cynddelw's work shines the force of his proud personality exulting in his rich command of language.

Hywel ab Owain Gwynedd

Hywel was an illegitimate son of the king of Gwynedd by an Irish mother, and was active in military campaigns from the 1140s onwards. He was killed in battle against his half-brothers after his father's death in 1170. His work is the earliest example of love poetry in Welsh, predating that of Cynddelw by a few years, but there is good reason to believe that he was heir to a now-lost native

Hywel ab Owain Gwynedd

A love lyric

I love the trampling of a horse in summer time,
Keen are the soldiers before a brave lord.
The swift-flowing wave is topped with foam,
The apple-tree has put on a new aspect.
My shield shines on my shoulder ready for combat;
I loved – I never had her despite desire –
A tall white hemlock, gentle and tender inclination,
Of the same colour as bright sunlight at midday,
Delicate shining form, soft, white, clear,
Hardly does a reed bend at her step.
Little darling of tender nature,
She is hardly older than a ten-year-old girl.
Child-like, shapely, full of comeliness,
She was taught as a child to give freely.
Child-woman, ardour embraces the beauty more readily
Than unseemly speech from her mouth.
Petitioner on foot, will I have a tryst?
How long will I beseech you? Stick to your task.
Love's madness has left me helpless,
Jesus will not blame me, He who knows.

tradition. Six poems have survived by him, five of them short love lyrics and the other a *Gorhoffedd*, or boast, a genre also attested in the work of his contemporary Gwalchmai ap Meilyr. Hywel's *Gorhoffedd* is divided into two sections, which may in fact be separate poems, the first expressing his love of his native land of Meirionnydd, apparently written when he was on a diplomatic expedition to Scotland, and the second boasting of the women he has loved, of whom nine are mentioned by name. His love poems also give passionate expression to his masculine delight in women, nature, and martial prowess, and their strong sensuality is heightened by the sharp sense of unsatisfied desire. Hywel's work was composed as sophisticated entertainment for a courtly audience, and parallels that of his contemporaries in Provence such as Bertran de Born.

The court poets of Gwynedd

Gwynedd was the most powerful of the three Welsh kingdoms, and it is understandably the best represented in the poetry. Gwynedd's strength was re-established by Gruffudd ap Cynan towards the end of the eleventh century, and it was during his reign that the flowering of court poetry first became apparent in the work of Meilyr Brydydd, who sang an elegy on Gruffudd's death in 1137. As already seen, the bardic tradition flourished at the court of his son Owain Gwynedd, but it was in the reign of Owain's grandson Llywelyn the Great, from the 1190s until 1240, that the kingdom was at the height of its fortunes. Llywelyn was fortunate to have a court poet commensurate with his greatness in Llywarch ap Llywelyn, nicknamed *Prydydd y Moch* ('the Poet of the Pigs'), who celebrated his achievements in a series of majestic *awdlau*. The court poetry of Gwynedd in the thirteenth century lacks the exuberance which characterized the twelfth-century poets, but the sombre mood reflects a mature political awareness, most notably in the work of Llygad Gŵr, who supported the ambition of Llywelyn ap Gruffudd to unite Wales under his leadership after 1267. Llywelyn ap Gruffudd's death at the hands of the English in 1282 marked the end of Welsh political independence, and the fateful significance of the event was recognized in two elegies by Gwynedd poets, one a stoical statement of human tragedy by Bleddyn Fardd, and the other a sweepingly rhetorical vision of cosmic disaster by Gruffudd ab yr Ynad Coch, which is surely the most powerful elegy in the Welsh language.

Gruffudd ab yr Ynad Coch

from 'Elegy for Llywelyn ap Gruffudd'

The heart's gone cold, under a breast of fear;
Lust shrivels like dried brushwood.
See you not the way of the wind and the rain?
See you not oaktrees buffet together?
See you not the sea stinging the land?
See you not truth in travail?
See you not the sun hurtling through the sky,
And that the stars are fallen?
Do you not believe God, demented mortals?
Do you not see the whole world's danger?
Why, O my God, does the sea not cover the land?
Why are we left to linger?
There is no refuge from imprisoning fear,
And nowhere to bide – O such abiding! ...

Cantref and township, all are invaded,
Every lineage and clan slips under.
The weak and the strong were kept by his hand,
It is every cradled child that screams.
It did me no good, so to deceive me,
When his head was off, to leave me mine.

The Poets of the Gentry

The demise of the independent princes constituted a crisis for the
Welsh bardic order. An element of continuity was provided by the
patronage of the Welsh church, which had long been supportive of
the native literary culture. But the place of the princes as patrons of
the poets was taken mainly by the native gentry (*uchelwyr*), a
land-owning class which flourished under English rule by holding
offices in local government. As a result of this shift the poets
suffered a loss of social status since they no longer had their
privileged position in the royal courts. Poets could not be
maintained by the gentry on a permanent basis, and so they were
forced to adopt the practice of travelling the country from one

noble house to another on bardic circuits, visiting their patrons especially at the major religious festivals. They were distinguished from itinerant minstrels by their elaborate training in the poetic craft and by their ability to confer the eulogy traditionally associated with the native aristocracy. But, on the other hand, they gradually adapted the style and matter of their poetry to make it more accessible and entertaining, probably influenced by lesser minstrels (known in Welsh as *y glêr*). From the fourteenth century onwards the relationship between poet and patron was a much more personal and informal one, the two often being of equal social status, and many noblemen took an active interest in the bardic craft, contributing an innovative spirit to the poetry of the period. With the aid of hindsight the loss of political independence can therefore be seen to have been ultimately beneficial to Welsh poetry in the later Middle Ages.

The so-called Bardic Grammars associated with the churchmen Einion Offeiriad and Dafydd Ddu of Hiraddug are evidence of moves to reorganize Welsh poetics in the fourteenth century, but they were certainly not used as practical textbooks in training poets, and it is unclear how much influence they actually had on bardic practice. The most significant innovation in poetic form, which paved the way for a new style, was the development of the *cywydd* metre. The *cywydd* was much simpler than the traditional metres of the *awdl*, consisting of couplets of seven-syllable lines, with end-rhyme alternately stressed and unstressed. Since the rhyme changed with each new couplet the metre had a much lighter effect and greater flexibility, well-suited for description and for recounting an amusing story. The *cywydd* was probably too simple to be used by the Poets of the Princes, but it was made more intricate in the fourteenth century by the addition of *cynghanedd* as compulsory ornamentation within each line. Of course, the *awdl* continued to be used until the end of the medieval period, but by the fifteenth century the *cywydd* had become established as the standard form for all types of poetry, so that the poets of the period are often referred to in Welsh as *Cywyddwyr*.

Cynghanedd
The term *cynghanedd* means literally 'harmony', and it refers to the complex system of sound correspondences which adorns Welsh strict-metre poetry. *Cynghanedd* is entirely unique to Welsh, and is still a flourishing art today. It developed gradually over centuries of

bardic practice, and did not become a formal system with strict rules until the fourteenth century. Its ramifications are far too intricate to be explained in full here, but the basic principles can be demonstrated with the help of an illustrative passage from Lewys Glyn Cothi's elegy for his five-year-old son Siôn:

> Afal pêr ac aderyn
> A garai'r gwas, a gro gwyn;
> Bwa o flaen y ddraenen,
> 4 Cleddau digon brau o bren.
> Ofni'r bib, ofni'r bwbach,
> Ymbil a'i fam am bêl fach.
> Canu i bawb acen o'i ben,
> 8 Canu 'wo' er cneuen.
> Gwneuthur moethau, gwenieithio,
> Sorri wrthyf fi wnâi fo,
> A chymod er ysglodyn
> 12 Ac er dis a garai'r dyn.

(The lad loved a sweet apple and a bird and white pebbles; a bow made of a thorn branch, a flimsy wooden sword. He feared the pipe, he feared the bogey, he would beg his mam for a little ball. He would sing a note from his mouth to everyone, he would sing 'oo-o' for a nut. He would fondle and flatter, and sulk with me, and then make up for a bit of wood and for a dice which the boy loved.)

There are four main types of *cynghanedd*. The simplest is *cynghanedd lusg*, in which the penultimate syllable of the last word in the line rhymes with the end of a word earlier in the line. Examples can be seen in lines 1, 3 and 11 above, where the relevant syllables are underlined. Consonantal correspondence is essential to two types, *cynghanedd groes* and *cynghanedd draws*. The simpler of the two is *cynghanedd draws*, in which the same sequence of consonants is repeated at the beginning and end of the line, with a section in between which is not part of the correspondence. There is an example in line 9, where the stressed syllables in each half of the line are underlined, each having the sequence *n-th* preceded by a *g*. Line 8 contains another, where the absence of a consonant after the stressed syllable is part of the correspondence. In *cynghanedd groes* the two halves of the line match completely, with no consonants left out in the middle. An example can be seen in line 5, again with stressed syllables underlined, and others in lines 2, 6, 7 and 12 (note that the stressed words never end with the same consonant). *Cynghanedd sain* is a combination of rhyme and consonantal correspondence. The line is divided into three parts, the first and second being linked by rhyme and the second and third by alliteration, as seen in lines 4 and 10.

Cynghanedd may appear at first sight to be a very restrictive and artificial system, but in fact it is not so at all in the hands of a skilled practitioner. The four main types outlined above can be further subdivided according to various possible stress patterns, giving plenty of scope to avoid rhythmic monotony. More importantly, *cynghanedd* is intended to be appreciated by the ear of the listener, not to be analysed on the page. It is essentially a matter of emphasizing the main stressed syllables in the line, and if the poet is a master of his craft then the *cynghanedd* will always serve to highlight the sense, often giving the line a memorable epigrammatic quality. Any translation of Welsh strict-metre poetry must always be woefully inadequate because of the complete loss of this essential feature.

Dafydd ap Gwilym
The outstanding innovator of the fourteenth century was Dafydd ap Gwilym, who is regarded by many as the greatest Welsh poet of any period. Dafydd was apparently not a professional poet, but the bardic tradition was strong in his family, which had served the Norman administration in south-west Wales for generations, and he learnt the poetic craft from his uncle, who was constable of Newcastle Emlyn. His dates are still a matter for conjecture, but it seems that he died young, and his period of activity was probably in the 1340s and 1350s. Some one hundred and fifty of his poems have survived, a remarkably large corpus which is an indication of the wide popularity of his work. A few are religious and praise poems which show him to have been a master of the traditional style, but the vast majority are love poems in the *cywydd* metre. Dafydd is generally credited with having pioneered the development of the *cywydd*, and his work certainly ensured the spread of its popularity. Some of the themes of his love poetry are anticipated by a few of the later *Gogynfeirdd*, but Dafydd was the first to develop a form wholly appropriate to the new subject matter.

Dafydd ap Gwilym seems to have been particularly receptive to the continental literary influences which were reaching Wales at this time, and also to the stimulus of popular culture, blending both into the native literary tradition to create a radical new synthesis. His treatment of nature is a case in point. Dafydd certainly draws on the close association between nature and love which had existed in Welsh poetry since at least the twelfth century, with symbolic use of scenes from nature forming a correlative to human desires. To this is added on the one hand the folk custom of seasonal celebration, particularly on the coming of summer in the month of May, and on the other hand the European literary convention of the secluded woodland spot as the ideal setting for a love-tryst. And the vivid detail of his descriptions of scenes and creatures makes nature much more than just a conventional backdrop for love in his work. His descriptions are enlivened by the technique of *dyfalu*, which consists of a series of imaginative metaphors following one another with kaleidoscopic effect, so that fog becomes a parchment-roll, a grey cowl, and a mail-coat hanging heavy on the earth. Dafydd's empathy with nature is at its strongest in his *llatai* poems, in which wild creatures, and even on one occasion the wind, are sent as love-messengers.

Dafydd sang of his love for various women, but two in particular stand out as the main subjects of his poetry, Morfudd and Dyddgu. Morfudd is known to have been the wife of an Aberystwyth merchant nicknamed *y Bwa Bach*, and Dafydd's many poems to her show that they had a long-lasting love affair both before and after her marriage. Dyddgu was the daughter of a Cardiganshire nobleman, unattainable because of her high social status. Although they were real women, Dafydd's relationship to these two nevertheless corresponds to opposing concepts of love in European literature, Morfudd being the faithless young wife of the *fabliau* tradition, to be won from her mean old husband by the wily poet, and Dyddgu the ideal lady of courtly love, who can only be admired from afar.

Perhaps Dafydd ap Gwilym's greatest contribution to the Welsh poetic tradition was to make himself the main subject of his poetry. With the important exception of Hywel ab Owain Gwynedd, the court poets had composed in a fundamentally impersonal and objective mode. Dafydd's poems are entirely subjective, based on his own feelings and experiences, and he was very ready to generate humour at his own expense by playing the buffoon. A fine example is the poem 'Trouble at an Inn', in which Dafydd seduces a girl at an inn, arranging to come to her bed when everyone else is asleep, but stumbles over the furniture in the dark and wakes up three Englishmen, who take him for a thief. He ends up by sneaking ignominiously back to his own bed, begging God for forgiveness.

And yet his self-mockery often has a serious edge to it, accompanied by a profound awareness of the pity and transience of human life. One of his most moving poems is a meditation on a ruined house

Dafydd ap Gwilym
'The Seagull'

Truly, fair seagull on the tide,
the colour of snow or the white moon,
your beauty is without blemish,
fragment like the sun, gauntlet of the salt sea.
You are light on the ocean wave,
swift, proud, fish-eating bird.
There you'd go by the anchor
hand in hand with me, sea lily.
Fashioned like a piece of shining paper,
you are a nun on the tide's crest.

Perfect image of a girl, you are praised far and wide,
make for the bend of a rampart and castle
and look, seagull, if you may see
a girl of Igraine's hue on the fine fortress.
Say my heartfelt words,
let her choose me, go to the girl.
Should she be alone, make bold to greet her,
handle the refined girl carefully
to gain advantage; say that I can't
(sensitive lad that I am) live unless I have her.

I love her with the full force of passion,
ah, men, never Myrddin,
with his fine flattering lip, nor Taliesin,
did love a prettier girl.
Sought-after like Venus, copper-haired,
surpassing beauty of perfect form.

O seagull, if you get to see
the cheek of the fairest maid in Christendom,
unless I have the tenderest of greetings,
the girl will be my death.

where he once lay with his girl, and in another he foresees Morfudd's old age with nightmarish clarity.

Dafydd also made an innovative contribution to the praise tradition in a group of seven poems which he addressed to his friend and patron Ifor Hael of Glamorgan. In these he adapted the characteristic modes of love poetry to produce eulogy of a very personal and intimate kind. He was probably the first to use the *cywydd* for praise poetry, and his portrait of the close relationship between poet and patron was to be highly influential. It was Dafydd who gave Ifor the name 'Hael' ('the Generous'), and under that name he became the most famous of all patrons of Welsh literature.

Iolo Goch

A younger contemporary of Dafydd ap Gwilym, Iolo Goch played a vital role in adapting the praise tradition to the new social circumstances, following Dafydd's lead in employing the *cywydd* metre but giving it the dignity of the traditional modes of eulogy, the vocabulary, the imagery, and the high ideals of social responsibility. His more conservative approach tempered the radicalism of Dafydd ap Gwilym and ensured the essential continuity of the Welsh poetic tradition in this period of transition. Iolo was a native of the Vale of Clwyd in north-east Wales, and seems to have been more dependent on the patronage of the nobility than Dafydd, travelling throughout Wales in a long career which spanned the second half of the fourteenth century. He addressed poems to some of the most powerful men in the country, including King Edward III, whom many of the Welsh gentry served in his wars in France and Scotland. Iolo's attitude towards the English rule in Wales was deeply ambiguous, at once resentful of foreign oppression (his own family seems to have lost hereditary land after the Edwardian conquest), and yet loyal to the Crown and keen for his patrons to participate in its government in Wales. Iolo experienced the devastation of the Black Death as a young man, and his poetry conveys an acute awareness of the danger of social disintegration and the need to preserve the established order.

Iolo's most famous patron was Owain Glyndŵr, to whom he addressed three poems in the late 1380s. Owain was a direct descendant of the princes of Powys, and he rose in rebellion against the English to claim his inheritance shortly after Iolo's death. One of Iolo's poems does express Owain's resentment at his disinheritance, but more characteristic of the poet's concern for social stability is his description of Owain's house and estate at

Sycharth. This is one of the earliest of many such descriptions of noble houses in the later Middle Ages, and the detailed materiality is one of the most appealing qualities of the poetry of the *Cywyddwyr*. The profound sense of order and interdependence symbolized by the architecture makes Iolo's poem a classical expression of the deeply conservative social ideal upheld by the landed gentry. The same ideal is expressed more indirectly in an unusual poem praising the ploughman for his humble devotion to his duty, probably a reflex of the anxiety caused by the Peasants' Revolt of 1381.

Iolo Goch was an extremely inventive poet who often used literary conventions in unusual ways to enliven his poetry. For instance, his account of a bardic circuit of south-west Wales is in the form of a dialogue between his body and his soul (a convention of religious literature), the soul having sought the drunken poet's body in the homes of all his patrons. His description of Cricieth Castle uses the device of the dream vision to give it the quality of an ideal romance court, echoing *The Dream of Macsen Wledig*. Such inventiveness is not just a personal characteristic, but rather a strength common to all the *cywydd* poets of the fourteenth century. The most notable example of all is the elegy by Llywelyn Goch ap Meurig Hen on the death of his sweetheart Lleucu Llwyd, which uses the convention of the serenade with poignant dramatic effect, the poet appealing to his love to open the door of the grave and rebuking her for her silence, just as the serenading lover would do.

Fifteenth-century poetry

The disruption caused by Owain Glyndŵr's rebellion inevitably affected the bardic order in the early fifteenth century, but from the 1430s onwards the tradition flourished as never before. The eisteddfod held at Carmarthen in about 1451 is an indication of the revival of culture, bringing together poets and musicians from all parts of Wales, and providing the occasion for a revision of the rules of the poetic craft. The chair for poetry was won by Dafydd ab Edmwnd, a nobleman from Flintshire who illustrates the major contribution made by amateur poets to the tradition in this period. The *cywydd* form was by now well established, and poets such as Guto'r Glyn, Dafydd Nanmor, Lewys Glyn Cothi, and Gutun Owain display a complete mastery of their medium. They perhaps lack the innovative spirit of the previous century, but they express themselves in an easy and natural style which belies the intricacy of their craft. They are polished classical artists celebrating the joys of

byr angel hawd i beler.
Aphwyr hael ymddwyf lan ffror.
Imroedl ytt gif chariat.
Hemr lev hanner yslat.
Mab jeu vchan byt nal.
Dy dridieu o baer oaer idwal.
kariat or tut ac or tair.
Zyverkbdr ir kydirieit.
Blaenbdr lle gynawt vaevadr dellt.
Bua elnael abuellr.
Bedoyr gruffuth ap addni.
Bybyt no i uab dy uam.
Deyrhw adrha yn deu.
Dann tair ar dar y reidieu.
y buymn coch a oleyn herd.
Bryn hengorf a breulmigeed.
Bryn yr aur melyn ar mel.
Bryn iach dan bybren uchel.
Bryn mil hawon vehelyth.
Bryn y beird ar barneu lyrh.
I nard ac i onerdyu.
A mi er ioet kymryv mryn.
Poy ar gynaeth yn uab maeth mel.
Poy mdogon ap ho.
jen i uab munnol.

A page from one of Lewys Glyn Cothi's manuscripts (Peniarth 109).

an aristocratic civilization in graceful and witty poetry. Although their work is basically uniform in terms of style and vision, nevertheless the personality of each individual poet is strongly present in his poems, the genial humour of Guto'r Glyn contrasting with Dafydd Nanmor's meditative appreciation of stability. Like his teacher Dafydd ab Edmwnd, Gutun Owain was a gentleman-poet, a connoisseur of bardic learning who in some ways anticipates the Renaissance humanists. Lewys Glyn Cothi's warm humanity is seen in the moving elegy which he composed on the death of his five-year-old son Siôn, from which an extract is quoted above as an illustration of *cynghanedd*. Lewys's work is the largest surviving body of medieval Welsh poetry, he being one of the first of the bards to preserve his own work in writing, rather than relying on oral transmission.

The most characteristic genre of the period is the request poem (*cywydd gofyn*), in which the poet would ask a patron for a gift (such as a horse, a weapon, or a garment), sometimes for himself but more often on behalf of another nobleman. The gift would be described in elaborate detail using the technique of *dyfalu* already seen in the work of Dafydd ap Gwilym. This is social poetry at its best, celebrating both the craftsmanship of the maker (divine or human) and the bonds of friendship symbolized by the gift-giving. Other conventions such as the elegy and the descriptive love poem were also employed with great sophistication in this period. The classical poetry of the fifteenth century reached its climax in the work of Tudur Aled (*c.* 1465–1525), a virtuoso craftsman who achieved a remarkable density of ornamentation and imagery over the whole range of poetic genres.

Dissident voices

The image of a stable and contented society presented by the praise poetry of the later Middle Ages was of course a selective one, and did not go unchallenged. Discontent at oppression by the English was widespread, and was given covert but ferocious expression in the notoriously obscure *cywyddau brud*, prophetic poems which drew on a long tradition of vaticination in Welsh and made use of the animal symbolism of Geoffrey of Monmouth's Merlin prophecies. These found fertile ground in the turmoil of the Wars of the Roses, supporting Welsh hopes of regaining their lost sovereignty by claiming the throne of Britain. The prophetic tradition came to an end with the fulfilment of those hopes when the Welshman Henry Tudor was crowned king in 1485, although the political consequences of that event for Wales were very different from the apocalyptic visions of the prophecies.

Another sharp contrast to the untroubled idealism of the praise poetry was the derisive nihilism of satire (*dychan*), an elaborate form of invective or curse which was part of the traditional repertoire of the Celtic poet and was widely feared as a potentially lethal weapon. Mock flytings between poets were often staged as entertainment in medieval Wales, and bardic contentions sometimes involved disputes about the nature and purpose of poetry. But satire was occasionally used in deadly earnest against a nobleman who refused to fulfil his duty of generosity towards the poets. Whether or not the victim's health was affected is not known, but his social standing undoubtedly suffered as a result of the poet's condemnation.

Dychan was an essentially conservative genre, based on accepted social values. A much more radical form of satire is found in the

Siôn Cent

from 'Man's Vanity'

The mighty warrior must suffer
the loss of a great forfeit,
and leave, there's no avoiding it,
a mute man's wealth on the ground.
He will get a secure shirt,
bitter sort, of less than six feet,
and set off for the crowded churchyard
on his horse towards the cold grave.
After wine the beloved kinsman
will be put diligently into the earth,
and his kin will mourn him for a while
as he is covered with a spade.
Cruel tormentor, does the man not know,
grim task, that no border
supports his house there, awful abode,
except the earth alone?
And the heavy earth weighs down,
and gravel presses against the cheek.

work of Siôn Cent, an amateur poet from the border region of south-east Wales, who was probably active in the aftermath of the Glyndŵr rebellion in the early fifteenth century. Using a direct and vigorous style clearly influenced by populist preachers, Siôn Cent's poems are powerful sermons on the vanity of all worldly things, reminding his audience of mortality by graphic descriptions of death and the grave. In a contention with Rhys Goch Eryri he denounced the sinful falsehood of the bardic muse, and his work as a whole tended to undermine the very premises of eulogy by condemning all the marks of worldly status celebrated by the poets.

Women seem to have been completely excluded from the bardic order, and as a consequence medieval Welsh poetry presents a male-orientated view of the world, emphasizing patriarchal social values and militaristic virtues. A few women did apparently master the craft, but the only one by whom a substantial corpus of poems has survived is Gwerful Mechain (*fl.* 1460–1500). Gwerful is notorious for some remarkable poems in celebration of female sexuality, and she did engage in salacious exchanges with male poets, but her work as a whole is wide-ranging, including religious verse and a spirited defence of women. It is a great pity that no collection of her work has yet been published, since she is to be valued as the only voice speaking on behalf of women in medieval Wales.

The decline of the bardic order

From about the middle of the sixteenth century onwards there was a marked decline in the standard of strict-metre poetry. The last major poet of the medieval tradition was Wiliam Llŷn, who died in 1580. Of course, the tradition lasted longer in some areas than others, such as the mountainous region of Ardudwy where the Phylip family maintained the old bardic practices well into the seventeenth century. Siôn Phylip's *cywydd* describing a seagull is particularly admired. But poets found it increasingly difficult to make a living from their craft, and by the end of the seventeenth century the professional bardic order had ceased to exist. The main causes of the decline were certainly social ones, primarily the Anglicization of the Welsh gentry in the Tudor period, which deprived the poets of a good deal of their patronage. On the other hand, the innate conservatism of the bardic order itself made it difficult for the poets to adapt to the more fluid social order and the new print culture of the Renaissance. But the disappearance of the medieval bardic order did not result in a complete break in the poetic tradition. As will be seen, the essentials of the craft were passed on to amateur practitioners, the poet continued to play a central role in Welsh society, and the verbal artistry of medieval poetry has been a source of inspiration to Welsh writers ever since.

5 The Renaissance

Humanism

The Renaissance was a European movement whose influence reached Wales through England from about 1540 onwards. Renaissance humanism was based on admiration for the classical learning of the Greek and Latin languages, and the humanists' aim to ensure the spread of that learning was facilitated by the development of the printing press in the fifteenth century. Although Wales was hindered from participating fully in the new print culture by the lack of the court and urban society necessary to maintain it, the Welsh humanists were nevertheless very anxious to take advantage of the printing press, feeling that their language was in danger of being left behind. The first to publish a book in Welsh was Sir John Price, whose collection of basic religious texts known as *Yn y lhyvyr hwnn* came out in 1546. But the true pioneer of publishing in Welsh was William Salesbury of Denbighshire, whose intellectual interests were given an urgency of purpose by his radical Protestantism. The breadth of his learning is typically humanist, his publications in both Welsh and English covering linguistics, proverbs, science, law and religious controversy, but his overriding aim was to activate the resources of the Welsh language in preparation for the translation of the scriptures.

Just like those of other countries, the Welsh humanists felt that their language was much inferior to Greek and Latin, and needed to be improved if it was to encompass the new learning. Their main activity was therefore in the field of linguistic scholarship, compiling dictionaries to enrich the vocabulary and grammar books to establish standards of correct usage, and studying rhetoric in order to bring the felicities of classical style into Welsh. William Salesbury made a start with his Welsh–English dictionary of 1547, but the first major work was the grammar by the Catholic exile Gruffydd Robert, published in Milan from 1567 onwards. Composed in a lively dialogue form and containing passages of elegant Ciceronian prose, it was itself a contribution to the new literature for which it sought to lay the foundations. Another scholar with personal experience of Italian humanism was Dr Siôn

William Salesbury

Appeal to the Welsh people

Why do you let your books mould in corners, and rot in chests, and conceal them from everyone's sight except your own? Because you conceal the old books of your language, and especially those of the holy scripture, there is no Welshman alive, however learned he be, who can express the holy scripture properly in Welsh, with the poor language which you commonly prattle in this age. Do you think that there is no need for different words, or a greater variety of expressions to propound learning and to discuss philosophy and arts, than is used by you in everyday conversation for buying and selling, eating and drinking? And if you think that then you are mistaken. And take this as a warning from me: if you do not rescue and reform and perfect the language in this present generation, it will be too late to do so afterwards. And if there is no learning, knowledge, wisdom, and godliness in a language, is it any better than the chatter of wild birds or the roar of animals and beasts? ... But listen now to what I have to say to you, those who have no hope of mastering English or any other language with learning in it; listen (I say) to what I will tell you: unless you wish to become worse than animals (which were not born to understand like man) seek learning in your language. Unless you wish to be more unnatural than any nation under the sun, honour your language and those who honour it. Unless you wish to abandon Christ's faith altogether, to have nothing whatsoever to do with him, to forget and expunge all his will for ever, get the holy scripture in your language, as it was in the time of your happy ancestors the ancient Britons.

(From the introduction to the proverb collection *Oll Synnwyr Pen Kembero Ygyd*, 1547)

Dafydd Rhys, who sought to reveal to the world the glories of the Welsh language and its literature by publishing a treatise in Latin in 1592. The culmination of Welsh Renaissance scholarship was the definitive study of the classical language of the poets by Dr John Davies of Mallwyd in his grammar of 1621 and his Welsh–Latin dictionary of 1632.

The Welsh humanists differed somewhat from their European counterparts in their attitude towards their native culture and history. The myth propounded by Geoffrey of Monmouth about the settlement of Britain by Brutus of Troy furnished the Welsh people with a classical origin which native humanists vigorously defended against criticism by sceptical historians right through until the nineteenth century. A related myth was that of a golden age of Welsh learning, associated with the druids referred to by classical authors. The books in which that learning was enshrined were believed to have been destroyed (including a reputed early Welsh translation of the Bible), but the myth inspired Welsh humanists to search for medieval manuscripts in the hope of finding some vestige of the glorious past. The bardic poets of the sixteenth century were regarded as the inheritors of that learned tradition, and the humanists' ambivalent attitude towards them was a combination of typically Renaissance contempt for the restrictive professionalism of the Middle Ages on the one hand, and, on the other, native pride in an ancient art equal to that of classical literature.

The ideological clash between humanism and bardism is epitomized by the poetic contention of fifty-four *cywyddau* exchanged between the Cambridge-educated Edmund Prys, archdeacon of Merioneth, and the professional poet Wiliam Cynwal from 1581 to 1587. Prys's contribution to the debate reads like a humanist manifesto for poetry, condemning the immorality of bardic praise and urging Cynwal to draw his material from the new learning. Cynwal's response is disappointingly negative, concentrating on Prys's lack of bardic qualifications, and is typical of the poets' failure to rise to the challenge of the Renaissance. Edmund Prys is a model of the sort of amateur poet which the humanists hoped to create by their treatises on poetry, but with this and a few other exceptions the strict metres remained the preserve of the professionals.

The Welsh Bible
It was in the Welsh Bible that humanism and Protestantism complemented one another most effectively. The translation can be regarded as the greatest achievement of Welsh humanism, in that the Bible was considered the foremost learned book, ensuring the

Llyfr Prophvvydoliaeth Esay.

PENNOD. I.

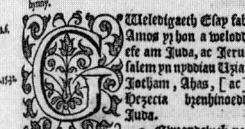

Aniolcharwch a chyndynrwydd y bobl. 11 Eu llygredic wasanaeth i Dduw. 14 A dialedd Duw am hynny.

GWeledigaeth Esay fab Amos yr hon a welodd efe am Iuda, ac Ierusalem yn nyddiau Uzia, Iotham, Ahas, [ac] Hezecia brenhinoedd Iuda.

2 Gwrandewch nefoedd, clyw dithe ddaiar, canys yr Arglwydd a lefarodd: megais, a meithrinais * feibion, a hwynt a wrthryfelasant i'm herbyn.

3 Yr ych a edwyn ei feddiannudd, a'r asyn breseb ei berchennog: [ond] Israel nid edwyn, fy mhobl ni ddeall.

4 Och genhedlaeth bechadurus, pobl lwythog o anwiredd, hâd y rhai yr gyionus, meibion llygredic, gwrthodasant yr Arglwydd, dirmygasant Sanct Israel, [a] chiliasant yn ôl.

5 Iba beth i'ch tarewir mwy? y cilwyrwch yn a chwanegwch: y pen oll [sydd] glwyfus, a'r holl galon yn llesc.

6 O wadn y troed hyd y pen, nid [oes] dim ynddo [onid] archollion, a chleisiau, a gweliau crawnllyd: [y rhai] ni wascwyd, ac ni rwymwyd, ac ni thynerwyd ag olew.

7 Y mae eich gwlad yn anrhaithiedic, eich dinasoedd wedi eu llosci â thân, eich tir a dieithriaid yn ei ysu yn eich gŵydd, ac wedi ei anrheithio fel yr ymchwelir estroniaid ef.

8 A merch Sion a adewir megis lluest yn y winllan, megis llety mewn gardd cucumerau, megis dinas warchaedic.

9 Oni buase i Arglwydd y lluoedd adel i ni megis ychydig weddill: fel Sodoma y buasem, a chyffelyb fuasem i Gomorra.

10 Gwrandewch air yr Arglwydd tywysogion Sodoma: clywch gyfraith ein Duw ni pobl Gomorra.

11 Beth [a fuddai] lliosogrwydd eich aberthau i mi medd yr Arglwydd? llawn ydwyf o boeth aberthau hyrddod, ac o frasder [mistiliaid] lloegstion: * gwaed bustych hefyd, ac

wyn, a bychod ni ewyllysiais.

12 Pan ddeloch i ymddangos ger fy mron, pwy a geisiodd hyn ar eich llaw [sef] sathru fy llysoedd?

13 Na chwanegwch ddwyn offrwm yn ofer, arogl-darth sydd ffiaidd gennif: ni allaf oddef [eich] newydd-loerau na'r Sabbothau gan gyhoeddi cymanfa, ac uchel-wyl [canys] anwiredd [ywynt.]

14 Eich lleuadau newydd, a'ch gwyliau gosodedic a gasaodd fy enaid, y maent yn faich arnaf, blinais yn eu dwyn.

15 A phan estynnoch eich dwylo y cuddiaf fy llygaid rhagoch: hefyd pan weddioch lawer ni wrandawaf: * eich dwylo ywynt lawn o waed. Esay.59.3.

16 Ymolchwch, ymlanhewch, bwriwch ymmaith drwygioni eich gweithredoedd oddi ger bron fy llygaid: peidiwch a gwneuthur ddrwg.

17 Dyscwch wneuthur daioni, ceisiwch farn, cyfarwyddwch y gorthrymmedic, bernwch [gyd a'r] ymddifad, dadleuwch [tros] y weddw.

18 Deuwch yr awr hon, ac ymresymmwn medd yr Arglwydd, pe bydde eich pechodau fel porphor, ânt cyn wynned a'r eira, pe chochent fel scarlat, byddant fel gwlân.

19 Os mynnwch, ac os gwrandewch: daioni y tir a fwyttewch.

20 Ond os gwrthodwch, ac [os] anufyddhewch, â chleddyf i'ch yssic: canys genau yr Arglwydd ai llefarodd.

21 Pa wedd yr aeth y ddinas ffyddlawn yn buttain? cyflawn [fu] o farn, lletuodd cyfiawnder ynddi: ac yr awr hon lleiddiaid [sydd ynddi.]

22 Dy arian a aeth yn sothach, dy win sydd gymmysclyd o ddyfroedd.

23 Dy dywysogion [ydynt] gyndyn, ac yn gystrannogion â lladron, pob un yn caru rhoddion, ac yn dilyn gwobrau: ni farnant y ymddifad, achwyn y weddw ni chaiff ddyfod attynt.

24 Am hynny medd Arglwydd Dduw y lluoedd [sef] cadarn [Dduw] yr Israel: aha, ymgysurraf yn erbyn fyng-wrthwynebwyr, a dialaf ar fyng-elynnion.

25 Yna y ymchwelaf fy llaw arnat, ac a lofS ix.iii.   cat

status of the languages into which it was translated. It was also, of course, an essential part of the programme of the Protestant Reformation in Britain, making it possible for the people of Wales to achieve salvation by personal experience of God's word. It was this consideration which persuaded Parliament to pass a bill in 1563 ordering that the Bible be translated into Welsh. As in other European languages, the translation was the composite effort of scholars over several generations, made possible by the refinement of the language during the Renaissance period.

William Salesbury had already taken a first step with his version of the Lectionary entitled *Kynniver Llith a Ban*, published in 1551, and when the Welsh bishops were ordered to produce a translation it was natural that they should entrust the work mainly to him. Salesbury was supported by Bishop Richard Davies, whose palace at Abergwili was one of the few Renaissance courts in Wales. By 1567 only the New Testament was ready for publication, all Salesbury's work except for five epistles translated by Bishop Davies and the Book of Revelation by Thomas Huet. Salesbury alone was responsible for the translation of the Book of Common Prayer published in the same year. Bishop Davies's approach to translation was that of an evangelical Protestant, clarity taking precedence over literary elegance. Salesbury, however, was more concerned with dignity of style, which he sought to achieve by archaic diction, diversity of expression, and an idiosyncratic orthography designed to reveal the Latin origin of words. His humanism interfered with the religious purpose of his work, and the result was a translation which was virtually unusable for all but the scholar. 'No true Welshman's ear could bear to hear it', was the comment of one contemporary. This was a tragedy at the time, for beneath the superficial oddities his translation was of a very high standard, but it did at least provide an excellent basis for later translators.

The first full translation of the Bible into Welsh was published in 1588, the work of William Morgan, at the time parish priest of Llanrhaeadr-ym-Mochnant, who translated the Old Testament for the first time and thoroughly revised the New Testament to eradicate the unacceptable aspects of Salesbury's style. The language of Morgan's translation was based on the usage of the poets, at once contemporary and classical, natural and dignified. It was a crucial link ensuring the continuity of the literary language from the Middle Ages through to the modern period. Only minor corrections and standardization were necessary in the revised version published in 1620, probably the work of Dr John Davies of Mallwyd. That version has the status of a classic of Welsh literature, similar to the King James Bible in English, and it served as the foundation for a new tradition of religious writing in the seventeenth and eighteenth centuries.

Religious prose

Almost all the Welsh prose works produced by the Anglican Church were translations from either English or Latin, partly due to the urgent need for devotional material in Welsh, but also because of the Anglican tradition of conformity and acceptance of authority which left little room for personal opinion. The earliest translations undertaken during the Renaissance period were of scholarly works, intended to increase the sum of learned books in Welsh, such as Bishop Jewel's defence of Anglican doctrine in Latin, translated by Morris Kyffin as *Deffynniad Ffydd Eglwys Loegr* in 1595, or Huw Lewys's translation of a work of Christian philosophy by Miles Coverdale, *Perl mewn Adfyd*, published in the same year. As the Renaissance lost impetus the emphasis shifted away from learning towards works of a more practical kind intended to instruct the common people in the rudiments of the Christian faith. These translations employ a direct style which reflects the practice of reading aloud to family and servants in large households. Outstanding amongst the seventeenth-century translators was Rowland Vaughan of Caer-gai, a member of the lesser gentry and staunch Royalist who published eight works, the earliest and best known of which is *Yr Ymarfer o Dduwioldeb* (1630), a translation of Lewis Bayly's *The Practice of Piety*.

The Puritan opponents of the Anglican establishment put much more emphasis on the spiritual experience of the individual, and were therefore more inclined to compose original works rather than translate authoritative texts. The most accomplished and stimulating of the Welsh Puritan writers was Morgan Llwyd (1619–59). Llwyd's Puritanism was first acquired at Wrexham in the Anglicized border region, under the influence of Walter Cradock, but the literary resources necessary to give expression to his new religious experience were inherited from his family background in Merioneth, one of the strongholds of traditional Welsh culture in that period. He served as a chaplain with the Parliamentary army in the Civil War, and was profoundly influenced by its religious and political radicalism, particularly the belief in the imminence of Christ's second coming. His first three books were composed in

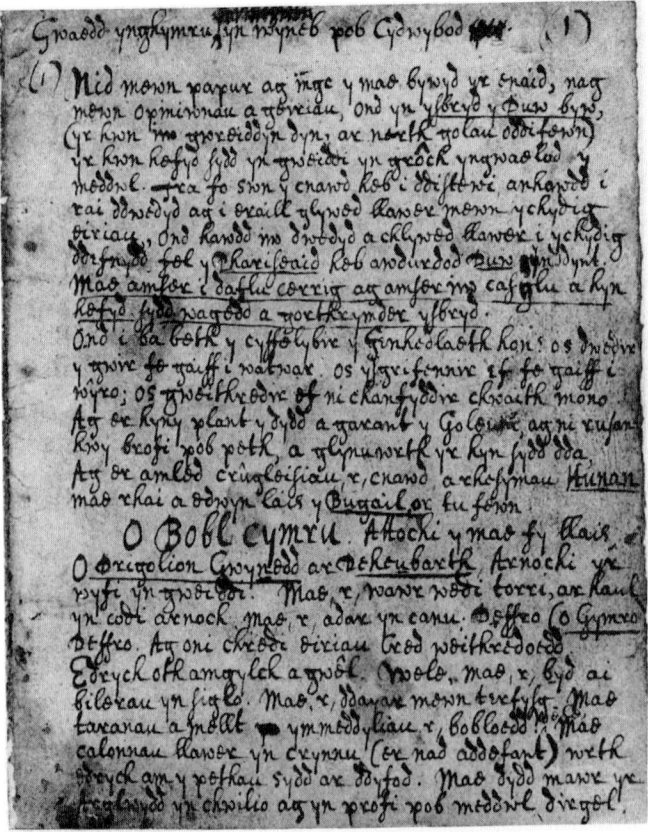

The first page of Morgan Llwyd's Gwaedd ynghymru, *in holograph.*

1653, during the Commonwealth period, when the calling of the Parliament of Saints convinced him that the millennium was about to begin, and all his work is coloured by his sense of living in exceptional times. In keeping with his ambivalent cultural allegiance he did publish three books in English, but his finest works were written in Welsh and were inspired by the urgent need to arouse his people from their spiritual slumber, as two of the titles show: *Llythur ir Cymru Cariadus* ('A Letter to the Beloved Welsh

52

People'), and *Gwaedd ynghymru yn wyneb pob cydwybod* ('A Cry in Wales to Every Conscience').

Morgan Llwyd's most important work is *Llyfr y Tri Aderyn* ('The Book of the Three Birds') of 1653. It is in the form of a dialogue between an eagle, a dove, and a raven, representing secular authority (perhaps Cromwell himself), the Puritan saints, and the Anglican establishment. The first third of the book consists of a lively debate between the three, in which the dove exposes the raven's worldly cynicism, and in the remainder the dove explains the mysteries of the spirit to the eagle. The central tenet of Llwyd's

Morgan Llwyd

The secret room

Dove.   There are many voices in man's heart. There is the sound of the world and its news, and its troubles, and its pleasures, and its terrors. Also within the room of the heart there is the sound of thoughts, and distempers, and the ebb and flow of flesh and blood. And thus the poor soul (like the drunkards' lodging) is full of clamour within, one desire squabbling with another, or like a fair or great market where din and chatter and hubbub fill the streets of the town within. This is why no man knows half his own thoughts, and cannot hear properly what his own heart is saying.

Eagle.   And how can man's mind attain peace?

Dove.   By going into the secret room: and that room is God himself within. But as long as you let the mind run out through the eyes and the senses, or look inwardly at pictures and images of things you have seen or remembered, the mind is like Lot leaving his house to reason with the Sodomites, until the Spirit of God plucks you in to converse with God in the room of the heart. And whilst the mind is like this outside, there is a devil inside preventing the thoughts from coming back in to God: and so the poor soul wanders away from home, seeing and desiring one thing after another outside, without seeing the God who is there within.

(From *Llyfr y Tri Aderyn*, 1653)

spiritual understanding, in which he was influenced by the German mystical writer Jacob Boehme, is the belief that God is present in every individual soul, and is to be approached by a process of turning inwards. He makes use of a wealth of metaphorical imagery to express this inner life of the spirit, and displays remarkable insight into the psychology of religious experience. Another key strength is his command of rhythm, ranging from the passionate rhetoric of the preacher to the quiet lyricism of the mystic, by which he succeeds in drawing the reader into the spiritual drama of his work.

The most exciting period of Welsh Puritan writing came to an end with the restoration of the monarchy in 1660, but concern for the spiritual condition of the Welsh people continued to motivate Puritan authors. Stephen Hughes was indefatigable in publishing morally improving texts on behalf of the Welsh Trust. One of his associates was Charles Edwards (1628–91?), the author of a classic of Welsh prose entitled *Y Ffydd Ddi-ffuant* ('The Sincere Faith'), which developed over three editions between 1667 and 1677 into a comprehensive work in three sections covering the history of the Christian faith in the world, the moral history of the Welsh nation (including an abridged version of Gildas's *De Excidio Britanniae*), and the spiritual condition of the individual Welshman. Edwards was of a more rationalist temper than Morgan Llwyd, but shared his capacity for illuminating metaphor. His work is highly significant as a statement of the influential belief that the Welsh were God's chosen people.

Free-metre poetry

'Free metres' is a term used in contrast to the bardic system of twenty-four strict metres. Most of the metres used are of native origin and are quite complex, distinguished from bardic poetry only by the absence of compulsory *cynghanedd* (although *cynghanedd* is used as optional ornamentation in some poems based on English song-tunes). It is far from certain that free-metre poetry was actually a product of the Renaissance, since poems such as the crude humorous rhymes of Robin Clidro (*fl.* 1545–80) may well belong to a medieval tradition, like the *hen benillion* discussed below, but the use of the free metres certainly flowered in the Renaissance period, and was encouraged by the Welsh humanists in order to make poetry more accessible to amateur practitioners.

As in England, the composition of love poetry was one of the attainments of a Renaissance gentleman, and numerous examples have survived by members of the Welsh gentry, such as the soldier and royal servant Richard Hughes (d. 1618). On the other hand, the impersonality of much of the free-metre poetry (in contrast to the personal relationship between bardic poet and patron) made it an ideal vehicle for social comment. The earliest protest poem in Welsh is the anonymous 'Coed Glyn Cynon' lamenting the cutting down of Glyn Cynon forest as fuel for the ironworks in sixteenth-century Glamorgan. The most prolific and accomplished free-metre poet of the seventeenth century was Huw Morus (1622–1709), a staunch Royalist whose social poetry upheld deeply conservative ideals. It was he who developed the use of *cynghanedd* in accentual metres, and his love poems and seasonal carols are aesthetically pleasing compositions, although somewhat devoid of intellectual content.

The principal subject of free-metre poetry in the Reformation period was of course religion. Verse was used by both Protestants and Catholics as an effective means of preaching the principles of the Christian faith to the common people, the most notable example being the immensely popular didactic verses of Rhys Prichard (1579–1644), vicar of Llandovery; these were published after his death by Stephen Hughes under the title *Canwyll y Cymry* ('The Candle of the Welsh'). Poets who were adept in the bardic strict metres sometimes chose to use the free metres in order to avoid the restrictions of *cynghanedd*, such as Edmund Prys in his metrical Psalter, *Salmau Cân*, of 1621, which has remained in use for congregational singing until the present day. Religious verse of a more personal and suggestive kind was composed by the Puritan Morgan Llwyd. It should be borne in mind that two of the outstanding religious poets of the English metaphysical school, George Herbert and Henry Vaughan, were Welshmen. Henry Vaughan was a Welsh-speaker, and even though he belonged to the Anglicized culture created by the Tudor Acts of Union, he was aware of the traditions of his people and drew inspiration from the landscape of his native Vale of Usk.

One type of free-metre poetry which was certainly not influenced by the Renaissance is the large body of folk-verse known as *hen benillion*, simple four-line stanzas recited to harp accompaniment. The verses were preserved orally, and collected from the seventeenth century onwards, but the tradition goes back to at least the sixteenth century, and probably to the Middle Ages. Although often highly personal, they are always anonymous, dealing with common human experience. Many project a female point of view, and it seems that women used this type of poetry more readily than the male-dominated strict metres. These succinct and suggestive verses have a powerful emotional force which has not been dulled by the passage of time.

Hen benillion

A selection of stanzas for the harp

Went to the garden to pick a posy,
Passed the lavender, passed the lily,
Passed the pinks and roses red –
Picked a nettle sting instead.

* * *

I'll go to the church next Sunday
And beneath the bellrope sit me,
And my eyes will be avoiding
Who is sitting next my darling.

* * *

Upon a flat stone by the shore
I told my love one word – no more;
Over it now thyme is growing,
And a few sprigs of rosemary blowing.

* * *

Only earth now, shroud and coffin,
Come betwixt me and my darling;
Oft I've gone a longer journey –
Never felt my heart so heavy.

* * *

I imagined when I married
Dance and song as much as I wanted.
All I got when I did marry –
A cradle to shake and lullaby baby.

(Translated by Tony Conran, *Welsh Verse*)

6 The Eighteenth Century

Gweledigaetheu y Bardd Cwsc

Ellis Wynne (1671–1734) of Y Lasynys near Harlech was educated at Jesus College, Oxford, and spent his life as a parish priest in his native district. He can be placed in the seventeenth-century tradition of Anglican translators, since he published a Welsh version of Jeremy Taylor's *The Rule and Exercises of Holy Living* in 1701, but his reputation rests on a work which aimed to improve the morals of his people by presenting a satirical picture of their sins, *Gweledigaetheu y Bardd Cwsc* ('The Visions of the Sleeping Bard') of 1703. Even in his masterpiece Wynne followed the contemporary practice of adaptation, drawing on two English versions of the Spanish satirical work *Los Suenos* by Quevedo (1627). His original contribution consisted in transplanting the satire into a Welsh context and strengthening its moral impact by arranging the dream visions into a coherent sequence in order to demonstrate the progress of sinners from this world to the next.

The three separate visions are of the World's Course (represented by three streets of a city, corresponding to the motives of pride, profit, and pleasure), of Death in his Nether Kingdom, and of Hell. The Sleeping Bard is guided throughout by an angel who serves to draw out the moral implications of the scenes observed. Before falling asleep the Bard is engaged in admiring the wide world through a telescope, but during the first vision he learns two crucial lessons: that the fair appearance of the world conceals its moral corruption, and that the Island of Britain under the Protestant monarch Queen Anne is a stronghold of the true faith in a satanic world. Wynne was a staunch Royalist whose most vicious satire was reserved for those who threatened the political and religious unity of Britain. His Lucifer is a burlesque figure who has trouble controlling some of the sinners in his realm, especially Oliver Cromwell!

Much of the appeal of Ellis Wynne's work for modern readers lies in his use of the colloquial Welsh of eighteenth-century Merioneth. However, Wynne did not use such a low style as a virtue in itself, but rather as a means of conveying contempt for the targets of his satire.

One of his great strengths was his ability to suit style to subject, including a dignified rhetoric inherited from Welsh Renaissance writers. His work has a graphic visual quality, presenting a vivid vision of a world peopled by memorably grotesque and garrulous characters. The specific subject matter of Wynne's satire is largely irrelevant today, and his intolerant conservatism and prejudices can be distasteful, but nevertheless the sharp wit and dramatic energy of his writing make this one of the most enduringly popular of the Welsh prose classics.

Drych y Prif Oesoedd

Theophilus Evans (1693–1767) was similar in many ways to Ellis Wynne, a country priest fiercely opposed to Nonconformity who devoted much of his writing to the Anglican cause in Wales. But his most important work, *Drych y Prif Oesoedd* ('The Mirror of the First Ages'), stands firmly in the Welsh humanist tradition of learning, representing the culmination of the nationalistic historiography of the Renaissance. Brought up in Newcastle Emlyn, he was influenced in his youth by a circle of Welsh scholars

Ellis Wynne
The gypsies' arrival in Hell

Presently twenty devils like Scotsmen with packs across their shoulders appeared and let them fall before the throne of despair and, on enquiry, what they carried turned out to be Gypsies. 'Ha!' said Lucifer, 'how did you know other people's fortunes so well, without knowing that your own fortune was leading you to this place?' There was not a word of reply with the astonishment of seeing here things more odious than themselves. 'Throw them,' said the king, 'with the witches in the upper shit-house, because their faces are so like the colour of faeces. There are no cats here or reed candles for them, but let them have a frog among them every ten thousand years if they're quiet, and don't deafen us with their jingle-jangle-clang.'

(from 'The Vision of Hell', translated by Gwyn Thomas, *Ellis Wynne*) in the Teifi Valley, and was only twenty-three when he published the first edition of his *Drych* in 1716, recounting the history of the Welsh people from the Tower of Babel to the death of Llywelyn ap Gruffudd. The revised second edition of 1740 is the work of a more accomplished story-teller, using graphic description and epic similes to convey the majestic drama of historical events. Evans drew on a variety of sources, and his work was influential in popularizing a number of key myths of Welsh history, such as the descent from Gomer, grandson of Noah (whence *Cymru*!), the link with Troy through Brutus, and the treachery of the Saxon leader Hengist and his daughter Rhonwen. His vision of history lacks the moral depth of Charles Edwards, but it was by far the most impressive narrative to be composed in Welsh since the Middle Ages.

Neo-classicism

The so-called Classical Revival of the eighteenth century can be seen as a continuation of the Renaissance ideal of bringing classical learning into Welsh literature. However, the crucial difference is that by the eighteenth century the medieval bardic tradition had completely come to an end. Rather than preserving or transforming old traditions, as earlier humanists had sought to do, the task now was one of recreating defunct traditions in a new form. The Welsh neo-classical authors were heavily influenced by their English counterparts of the Augustan period, and like them they took Greek and Latin classics as models, but the Welsh also had their own classical poetic tradition, which they avidly studied with the aid of the manuscripts and dictionaries bequeathed by the Renaissance scholars. 'Classical' thus had a double meaning in eighteenth-century Wales, referring to both foreign and native models. According to the principles of neo-classicism, literature was a social activity involving the expression of commonly accepted truths in perfect form, to be achieved by adherence to established rules of composition. These principles accorded very well with the nature of the Welsh poetic tradition with its emphasis on form and social function.

It was in the eighteenth century that London began to play an important role in Welsh literary life (a role which it continued to play to varying degrees until quite recently). The capital had attracted Welshmen since Tudor times and was the centre of Welsh publishing. Two patriotic societies established in London to promote Welsh culture (with a markedly antiquarian emphasis)

A portrait of Lewis Morris.

were the Cymmrodorion (1751) and the Gwyneddigion (1770). The prime movers of the Cymmrodorion Society were the Morris brothers of Anglesey, Lewis, Richard and William, three remarkable polymaths whose letters to one another provide a revealing picture of Welsh culture in the period. The most literary of the three was Lewis Morris (1701–65), an accomplished poet who wrote mainly light verse for the entertainment of friends, and a great encourager of poetic talents. Among his protégés were the pastoral poet Edward Richard (1714–77), the antiquarian Evan Evans (Ieuan Fardd, 1731–88), author of a well-known meditation on the ruins of Ifor Hael's court, and the greatest poet of the Welsh neo-classical movement, Goronwy Owen.

Goronwy Owen was born in Anglesey in 1723, the son of a tinker who had some grasp of the traditional poetic craft. Goronwy probably learnt the rudiments of the strict metres from his father, but after gaining a classical education at Friars School in Bangor he had more exalted literary ideals. He entered the church, but never managed to obtain a parish in Wales, and after years of poverty as a curate in England he eventually emigrated to America in 1757, where he died in 1769. All his important poems were written in the six years before he emigrated. The sum of his work is not great, and his literary ideals and the romantic myth of his life have been as influential as his poems themselves, but nevertheless he did succeed in giving memorable expression to a Christian philosophy of life. The bane of his poetic career, and that of generations of Welsh poets after him, was his ambition to compose an epic. He recognized that the strict metres were too restrictive for such a long composition, but his adherence to native models prevented him from following Milton's lead in adopting blank verse, despite his great admiration for *Paradise Lost*. The result was a bombastic *cywydd* of only 154 lines on the Day of Judgement, full of archaic vocabulary, which was excessively admired and imitated in the nineteenth century. Much more satisfactory are the urbane and lucid poems which he composed on the Horatian theme of the good life, such as the invitation to a fellow member of the Cymmrodorion Society to visit him at his home near London, which exhibits his skill in fashioning a polished epigrammatic couplet:

> Diwedd sydd i flodeuyn,
> Ac unwedd yw diwedd dyn.
>
> (There is an end to a flower,
> And just so is man's end.)

One of his most moving compositions is his stylized and yet poignant elegy on the death of his young daughter in 1755. But his finest work is his poem in praise of his native Anglesey, in which he

Goronwy Owen

from 'Praise of Anglesey'

When Môn and her gentle beauty
Shines red-hot from the heat of the flame,
And her bulging silver veins
And her lead and iron are aflame,
To what avails shelter from the molten earth?
May God provide a home for the soul!
A fine shining house of glory
In the fortress of the Stars, in the Holy choir;
And there chanting aloud
Their brilliant song to the beloved Lord,
May the Men of Môn be, and Goronwy,
Henceforth unable to take their leave.

(Translated by Branwen Jarvis, *Goronwy Owen*)

declares his poetic gifts to be subordinate to his office as priest. Although inspired by love of his homeland, he nevertheless places his personal feeling of *hiraeth* in the wider context of God's design through time and eternity.

Renaissance interest in the history and antiquities of Wales took on a new aspect in the eighteenth century. Whereas Renaissance scholarship was primarily concerned with the search for objective truth (a tradition which reached its climax with the publication of the first volume of Edward Lhuyd's *Archaeologia Britannica* in 1707), eighteenth-century antiquarianism was more creative, dealing with myths which sought to recreate the nation in a new romantic image. The most inventive antiquarian of the period was the Glamorgan stonemason and political radical Iolo Morganwg (Edward Williams, 1747–1826). In addition to creating the druidic pageantry of the Eisteddfod, much of Iolo's prodigious energy and imagination (stimulated by his addiction to laudanum) went into providing his beloved Glamorgan with the colourful literary inheritance which he felt it deserved. His influence was enormous, and it was not until the twentieth century that many of his claims were discredited. Condemnation of his shameless forgeries should not be allowed to obscure his standing as a writer of great vision and many voices who injected new life into Welsh literature. The science of lexicography also became a more creative enterprise in the work of William Owen Pughe, whose dictionary of 1803 contained large numbers of words of his own invention based on his belief that Welsh derived directly from the language of the patriarchs. Like Iolo Morganwg, his idiosyncratic ideas were extremely influential and gave an air of artificiality to much Welsh writing of the nineteenth century.

The Eisteddfod

An eisteddfod (from the verb *eistedd*, 'to sit') was originally a gathering of poets and musicians to regulate the affairs of their order. Such gatherings were held at very irregular intervals in the Middle Ages, the earliest known being that under the patronage of the Lord Rhys at Cardigan in 1176. Two important eisteddfodau were held at Caerwys in 1523 and 1567 in response to the crisis facing the bardic order at the end of the Middle Ages, but after that the tradition degenerated into informal meetings in taverns. The eisteddfod was revived as a competitive festival under the auspices of the Gwyneddigion Society in 1789, but it was not until the nineteenth century that major 'Provincial Eisteddfodau' came to be held regularly. By that time it had become associated with the neo-druidic ceremonies devised by Iolo Morganwg. Iolo's druidic assembly known as *Gorsedd Beirdd Ynys Prydain* was first held in conjunction with an eisteddfod at the Ivy Bush tavern in Carmarthen in 1819, and since 1858 it has been an integral part of the institution's pageantry, even though it has been exposed by modern scholars as entirely bogus. The modern National Eisteddfod first developed in the 1860s, and has been held annually since 1881, playing a valuable, if somewhat conservative, role in maintaining literary standards and providing Welsh authors with a national platform through its poetry, prose and drama competitions. It has been supported by a network of local eisteddfodau which have done a great deal to foster an active interest in literature amongst the common people. The Eisteddfod today is a lively and varied festival which acts as a focus for Welsh culture from the traditional to the avant-garde, and is an essential part of the literary life of the nation.

Popular culture

When the professional bardic order came to an end in the late seventeenth century the old poetic craft did not disappear entirely, but was passed on in a rather fragmentary form to amateur poets, mostly farmers and country craftsmen, known in Welsh as *beirdd gwlad* (literally 'country poets'). They fulfilled something of the social role of the old bardic order on a local scale, providing poems to mark significant events in the life of the community. The four-line *englyn* metre was still much used, but the command of *cynghanedd* was often rudimentary. Goronwy Owen's father, Owen Gronw, is an example of such a poet, and the cultural difference between him and his son indicates the split which occurred in the old poetic tradition between the learned and the popular. The two elements continued to enrich one another into the twentieth century, especially through the medium of the eisteddfod. The tradition of the *beirdd gwlad* reaches a very high level of artistry in the work of Robert ap Gwilym Ddu (1766–1850), a farmer who belonged to a circle of Caernarfonshire poets. His best-known poem is a passionate elegy on the death of his teenage daughter, which belongs to a genre running back through Goronwy Owen to medieval bards such as Lewys Glyn Cothi.

Popular entertainment was provided by ballads, recited and sold as pamphlets at fairs, which also functioned as a kind of news service. The melodies were mostly English, and the subject-matter ranged from sex to religion, but most popular were ballads about dramatic events of the day such as murders and shipwrecks. The ballad flourished in north Wales in the eighteenth century, and spread to the south with the Industrial Revolution, where it reflected the excitement caused by the social upheavals and radicalism of the period. The best balladeers were famous names whose work was in great demand, such as the blind harpist Richard Williams (Dic Dywyll), a sharp critic of social injustice who was a prominent agitator during the Merthyr Riots of 1831. The popularity of the ballad declined towards the end of the nineteenth century, killed off by Victorian respectability and the spread of the newspapers. Abel Jones (Bardd Crwst, 1829–1901) is generally regarded as the last of the great ballad-singers.

The interlude
The interlude (Welsh *anterliwt*) was a type of morality play in verse which was highly popular as entertainment for the common people in the eighteenth century, acted by small amateur companies touring the countryside. The basic story would be a well-known one, often taken from the Bible, and interwoven with it would be the farcical antics of two traditional characters, the Fool (complete

with phallus) and the Miser. The appeal of the interludes was probably due largely to the element of ribaldry, but they were also effective vehicles for moral lessons. The two would be combined in the advice to the girls in the audience, a standard feature of most

A portrait of William Williams Pantycelyn based on a sketch drawn from memory by an amateur artist.

interludes, warning against sexual laxity whilst describing it most suggestively. The interlude was also a vehicle for complaint about social oppression, targeting stock figures such as the steward and the lawyer. The foremost writer of interludes was Twm o'r Nant (Thomas Edwards, 1738–1810) of Denbighshire, a colourful personality with a bold and pungent poetic style. Nine of Twm's compositions have survived (as well as a good deal of poetry and a lively autobiography), dating from 1758 onwards. In his mature work, such as *Tri Chryfion Byd* ('The Three Mighty Ones of the World') published in 1789, the interlude takes on a new seriousness, dispensing with much of the traditional ribaldry, as the influence of Nonconformity began to be felt, adding moral depth to his social criticism. However, it was principally Methodist disapproval which led to the suppression of the interlude on the grounds of licentiousness in the early nineteenth century, along with many other folk customs.

The literature of the Methodist movement
The Methodist movement in Wales began with the preaching of Hywel Harris in 1735, and it was one of Harris's sermons which led in 1737 to the conversion of the greatest Welsh Methodist writer, William Williams (1717–91) of Pantycelyn in Carmarthenshire. In addition to his work as an itinerant preacher and organizer of Methodist societies, Williams Pantycelyn set about providing the movement with the literature which it needed, above all a body of hymnology. Between 1744 and 1787 he published eight collections of Welsh hymns, as well as two in English, the finest being those inspired by the great outbreak of religious enthusiasm centred on Llangeitho in 1762. The elegies which he wrote on the deaths of Methodist leaders such as Hywel Harris propounded the myth that Wales was in a state of spiritual darkness before the advent of Methodism, ignoring the preparatory work of earlier Nonconformists noted in the previous chapter. He also composed two epic poems, one a description of a Christ-centred universe in answer to Newtonian science, and the other an account of the spiritual development of a Methodist convert named Theomemphus. His numerous prose works aimed to provide spiritual guidance for converts, including a guide to marriage, *Ductor Nuptiarum* (1777), which is remarkable for its realistic handling of sexuality. Williams Pantycelyn stands in striking contrast to the classical poet Goronwy Owen, his prolific productivity completely unhindered by any concern for tradition or

formal models or correctness of diction. Williams had no pretensions to literary merit for its own sake, and yet his work is central to Welsh literature because it contains such a powerful expression of a spiritual movement which brought about a radical change in the culture of the Welsh people.

The main feature which distinguished early Methodism from other religious sects, whether Anglicans or Dissenters (or indeed Methodists of a later and more sober period), was its emphasis on the emotional aspect of religious experience. The key spiritual event was the conversion, the despairing realization of sinfulness giving way to joyful awareness of Christ's redeeming grace. The joy in itself was a sign of redemption, and hymn-singing was a means of giving expression to that joy, as well as serving to strengthen the bond of shared experience within a tightly-knit community of believers. Pantycelyn's hymns place great stress on the centrality of Christ's sacrifice, and adopt a personal viewpoint and vivid colloquial style in order to dramatize the relationship between the individual and Christ. They make extensive use of Biblical imagery, most importantly the Israelites' journey through the wilderness, which represents the life of the Christian in this world. The spiritual process continually re-enacted in hymn after hymn is that of turning away from worldly things towards Christ and longing for ultimate union with Him.

The second generation of Welsh Methodists sought to consolidate the gains of the eighteenth century and establish themselves as a socially respectable denomination. Great emphasis was placed on education, most notably in the work of Thomas Charles (1755–1814), who made Bala the main centre of Methodism in north Wales. In terms of knowledge of the literary language and tradition the most accomplished author of this generation was Thomas Jones (1756–1820), whose autobiography of 1814 is an important spiritual document. Another fine prose writer was Robert Jones of Rhos-lan (1745–1829), who produced a history of Methodism in Wales, *Drych yr Amseroedd* ('A Mirror of the Times') in 1820, which was a significant step in the development of the new Welsh identity as a Nonconformist people.

Hymnology continued to be an important aspect of Welsh poetry throughout the nineteenth century, but apart from Williams Pantycelyn the only hymn-writer whose work is still commonly read as literature is Ann Griffiths (1776–1805). Ann was born into a prosperous farming family at Dolwar Fach in Montgomeryshire, and in her youth she participated in the vigorous folk-culture of the

William Williams
I gaze across the distant hills

I gaze across the distant hills,
   Thy coming to espy;
Beloved, haste, the day grows late,
   The sun sinks down the sky.

All the old loves I followed once
   Are now unfaithful found;
But a sweet sickness holds me yet
   Of love that has no bound!

Love that the sensual heart ne'er knows,
   Such power, such grace it brings,
Which sucks desire and thought away
   From all created things.

O make me faithful while I live,
   Attuned but to thy praise,
And may no pleasure born of earth
   Entice to devious ways.

All my affections now withdraw
   From objects false, impure,
To the one object which unchanged
   Shall to the last endure.

There is no station under heaven
   Where I have lust to live;
Only the mansions of God's house
   Can perfect pleasure give.

Regard is dead and lust is dead
   For the world's gilded toys;
Her ways are nought but barrenness
   And vain are all her joys.

(Translated by H. Idris Bell, *The Oxford Book of
Welsh Verse in English*)

region. A fervent religious revival brought about her conversion to Methodism at the age of twenty with the rest of her family, and the remainder of her short life was devoted to God. She married in 1804, and died the following year shortly after the birth of a child. Her hymns were an expression of her personal spiritual experiences, and were not intended for congregational singing. Few were ever written down by her, but a number were recorded after her death from the memory of her illiterate maid servant, Ruth Evans, and first published in 1806. The work of Ann Griffiths belongs to a tradition of Methodist hymn-writing based on Biblical imagery and a firm grasp of Calvinistic theology, but her hymns are outstanding for their intense clarity of spiritual vision and their bold expression of the central paradoxes of the Christian faith. Comparison with the hymns of Williams Pantycelyn tends to reverse the stereotypical contrast between male intellect and female emotion, for the powerful religious feeling in her work is controlled by a remarkable intellectual detachment. But the overriding impulse of her hymns is the longing for complete union with Christ, and the way in which her early death appeared to fulfil that longing no doubt contributed to her awesome standing in Welsh Nonconformist culture. Ann Griffiths has traditionally had a unique status as the only important female writer in the history of Welsh literature before the twentieth century, but recent researchers have brought to light several neglected women (most notably Gwerful Mechain in the fifteenth century), and the precarious transmission of her hymns is no doubt indicative of the fate of many compositions by female poets in this period.

7 The Victorian Age

The nineteenth century was an extremely productive period in terms of publishing activity in Welsh, but literary standards were somewhat uneven. The reading public in Wales increased substantially, due largely to the influence of Nonconformity, which promoted literacy especially through the Sunday schools. The Industrial Revolution had a beneficial effect on Welsh culture, initially at least, by creating large Welsh-speaking communities in both north and south Wales which were able to support a flourishing periodical press. This is in stark contrast to the fortunes of Irish and Breton, which remained the languages of scattered rural communities. The invigorating effects of chapel and industry in Wales did have their negative side, however, in that they brought about a break with the culture of the past, whether deliberately, as in the case of Methodist suppression of the old folk-culture and disregard for secular traditions, or indirectly as a result of population movements away from the rural areas. By the Victorian period Nonconformity had ceased to be a radical spiritual force and had become a social institution which dominated Welsh culture and produced a stiflingly unworldly and pietistic literature. The most characteristic genre of the period was the biography (*cofiant*) of the preacher, weighty tomes glorifying the new folk-heroes. Another dominant institution in Welsh literary life was the eisteddfod, which certainly stimulated productivity and ensured fame for poets, but also promoted an unhealthy competitive spirit which saw the winning of prizes as the main purpose of literature.

Eisteddfod poetry
Much of the poetry produced by the eisteddfodau during the nineteenth century was inspired by Goronwy Owen's ideal of the Christian epic. Whilst Goronwy was acutely aware of the technical problems of composing an epic in the strict metres, later poets had no such qualms, producing lengthy odes (*awdlau*) in competition for the Eisteddfod Chair, many on didactic subjects such as 'Truth' or often about stirring events such as the Battle of Trafalgar. At its worst this poetry is entirely forgettable; long-winded, mechanical and bombastic. But at its best it can be a heroic display of poetic

will-power, containing impressive descriptive passages. The most highly-regarded of these eisteddfod odes is 'The Destruction of Jerusalem' by Eben Fardd (1802–63). Eben was only twenty-one when he wrote that poem; he continued to compete in eisteddfodau for the rest of his life, winning several chairs, but never achieved the same standard again. In the twentieth century, eisteddfod success is most often the beginning of a poet's career; in the nineteenth it was his highest accolade.

Around the middle of the nineteenth century there was a good deal of debate about the relative merits of the strict-metre ode and the *pryddest* in the free metres. For a time both were eligible for the Eisteddfod Chair, but in 1867 a separate competition was created for free-metre poetry, the Crown being awarded to the winning *pryddest*, as it is to this day. The *pryddest* allowed more freedom to develop theological themes, and the poets were heavily influenced by the model of Milton. Perhaps the finest of these free-metre epics is 'Iesu' ('Jesus') by Golyddan (1840–62), a work which was neglected at the time because it failed to win at the National Eisteddfod in 1860, but which has recently been acclaimed as one of the greatest Welsh poems of the nineteenth century. The sheer scale of these *pryddestau* is daunting for the modern reader, but it is a quality which was entirely characteristic of the ambitions of the age. The award for the longest poem in Welsh (and also one of the worst) must go to Gwilym Hiraethog's *Emmanuel*, published in two volumes in 1861 and 1867 and running to 22,000 lines.

In complete contrast to the long-winded epic poetry which dominated the eisteddfod was the succinct artistry of the *englyn* metre. Various forms of *englyn* had been used by Welsh poets since the Dark Ages, but towards the end of the Middle Ages the four-line *englyn unodl union* became established as a poem in its own right, and has continued to be one of the greatest strengths of Welsh poetics until the present day (for an example of the form see chapter 10). In the nineteenth century the *englyn* was popular amongst the *beirdd gwlad*, and in the hands of skilled exponents such as Trebor Mai (Robert Williams; read backwards his bardic name announces his Christian name) it has a pleasing lightness which avoids the pomposity of the more ambitious types of eisteddfod poetry.

Lyric poetry
The poetry of the eisteddfod was almost exclusively an impersonal mode, as had been the main stream of bardic poetry over the centuries. Personal feeling was far more prominent in the *hen*

71

benillion of the folk tradition and in the Methodist hymns, as already seen, and together with some influence from the English Romantics these provided the basis for the lyric poetry of the nineteenth century. Two pioneers of Welsh lyric poetry were Ieuan Glan Geirionydd (Evan Evans, 1795–1855) and Alun (John Blackwell, 1797–1841), both examples of the type of patriotic

Alun

'Song to the Nightingale'

When our dear earth is hid by night
    Under its black wing,
The woodland choir is mute, but you
    Then gently sing,
And if against your heart a thorn
    Throbs beneath your breast,
You, till generous day should break,
    Will but sing, and leave the rest.

And like you is this gentle girl,
    Partner more than rubies dear,
At sunset, though across the land
    A thousand clouds appear,
When all day's comforters are dumb
    Her fidelity's complete;
In the night's anguish and dismay
    Never sounded voice so sweet.

Though the worry almost numbs her heart
    She'll not complain
Nor tire her dear ones with distress –
    Her smile hides her pain;
Nor ends her song the long night through
    Until bright hope shall dawn,
Shining like an eye of gold
    Through the clear lids of morn.

(Translated by Tony Conran, *Welsh Verse*)

Anglican clergymen who made a vital contribution to Welsh culture in the first half of the nineteenth century. The work of Ieuan Glan Geirionydd is representative of the wide range of Welsh poetry in the period, including eisteddfod odes in the heroic style, a more successful meditative *cywydd* on the grave, some fine hymns, and lucid lyric poems, all expressing a stoical philosophy in the face of life's transience. He is one of the first Welsh poets to show appreciation of Wales's mountainous landscape for its own sake, as painters and tourists had already begun to do. A characteristic of the work of Alun and other lyric poets of the Victorian period is the idealization of the devoted wife, a tendency which was intensified in the second half of the century in response to the criticism of Welsh women's morals in the *Blue Books* report of 1847.

The outstanding lyric poet of the Victorian period was John Ceiriog Hughes (1832–87) of Dyffryn Ceiriog in Denbighshire. Ceiriog spent twenty years of his life working in Manchester; encouraged by a circle of Welsh poets there, he began writing poetry of *hiraeth* for the rural Wales of his youth, achieving enormous popularity with the publication of five volumes in the 1860s. His best-known work is the pastoral 'Alun Mabon', a sequence of songs

A sketch of the 1865 National Eisteddfod at Aberystwyth from Illustrated London News.

depicting a hill-farmer's simple existence and happy married life. The popular appeal of his work is partly due to his great gift for fitting words to traditional melodies. Most of his poems were composed as songs to be performed in concert halls and drawing rooms, and several are still popular today because of their melodious quality, such as 'Nant y Mynydd' ('The Mountain Stream'). But more essential was the way in which the sentimental and sanitized image of rural Wales offered in his work satisfied the emotional needs of the new Welsh middle class, many of them exiles who had been attracted to the cities of England and America in the age of the railway (it is quite appropriate that Ceiriog worked for a railway company in Manchester). In curious contrast to this idealization is the mockery of eisteddfod culture in his satirical fiction, 'The Correspondence of Sir Meurig Grynswth'. Ceiriog's work epitomizes a fundamental split in the Welsh psyche between the hard-headed materialism of the Victorian age, which identified with the dominant English culture, and soft-hearted attachment to

John Ceiriog Hughes
'What Passes and Endures'

Still do the great mountains stay,
    And the winds above them roar;
There is heard at break of day
    Songs of shepherds as before.
Daisies as before yet grow
    Round the foot of hill and rock;
Over these old mountains, though,
    A new shepherd drives his flock.

To the customs of old Wales
    Changes come from year to year;
Every generation fails,
    One has gone, the next is here.
After a lifetime tempest-tossed
    Alun Mabon is no more,
But the language is not lost
    And the old songs yet endure.

(Translated by Tony Conran, *Welsh Verse*)

Wales, which was confined to the emotional sphere and had no place in practical life. That split also became apparent in the poet's own life, since despite the *hiraeth* of his poetry he was in fact quite contented in Manchester, but when he decided to live up to his literary ideals and return to Wales as a stationmaster in 1868 he was bitterly disappointed by the reality of rural existence, missing the middle-class society of Manchester, and descended into alcoholism in the last years of his life.

Islwyn

The poetry of Islwyn (William Thomas, 1832–78) brings together two of the major impulses of the nineteenth century, religion and Romanticism. He was brought up near the village of Ynys-ddu in Gwent, and his first language was English, but he acquired a passionate interest in Welsh poetry, and his deep religious sensibility led him to train for the Methodist ministry. A crucial event in his life was the sudden death of his fiancée, Anne Bowen, in 1853. It was in response to that emotional crisis that he composed his major work over the following three years, two poems of some six thousand lines each, entitled 'Y Storm' ('The Storm'). Islwyn never sought to publish 'Y Storm' in full during his lifetime (his volume *Caniadau* of 1867 contains extracts), and editions after his death confused the two poems. It is only recently that the two have been published in their original form, although their standing as the greatest epic poetry in Welsh has long been recognized. Islwyn was clearly inspired by the mountainous landscape of his native country, and yet the essence of his poetic method is the mystical belief that all material things are but shadows of spiritual realities – 'To you my soul, what is the mighty thunder but an awesome image of His power?' His most famous and characteristic statement is, 'Mae'r oll yn gysegredig' ('Everything is sacred'). The storms described in dramatic detail are both natural and figurative, the internal weather of the soul on its pilgrimage through life. The violent moods of the first poem reflect his spiritual turmoil as he sought to come to terms with Anne's death, whilst the second is more meditative, clearly influenced by Edward Young's *Night Thoughts*. Throughout both poems themes are taken up and interwoven in a symphonic manner, with an impressive command of the varying rhythms of the long poem.

Islwyn subsequently cultivated a more classical approach to poetry, and attempted unsuccessfully to win eisteddfod laurels. Unfortunately, however, it was his mysticism which proved most

Daniel Owen.

influential, inspiring a school of poets known as Y Bardd Newydd (The New Poet), mostly Nonconformist ministers, who dominated the National Eisteddfod in the last decade of the nineteenth century. Welsh poetry can be seen to reach its lowest ebb in the work of men such as Iolo Carnarvon and Ben Davies, obscure metaphysical speculations in a formless and verbose style. The reaction against such barren stuff was one of the impulses behind the new movement in Welsh poetry at the beginning of the twentieth century.

The novel

The novel was rather slow in becoming established as a serious literary form in Welsh, due partly to the exceptionally high standing of poetry in Wales, to Nonconformist prejudice against fiction, and perhaps also to the lack of the middle-class urban readership which supported the novel in England, although there clearly was considerable demand for fiction in Welsh. The first work which might be considered to be a novel is Cawrdaf's *Y Bardd, neu y Meudwy Cymreig* ('The Poet, or the Welsh Hermit') of 1830, but it lacks the plot and characterization essential to the genre. Cawrdaf's work is openly moralistic in intent, as are the melodramatic stories inspired by the temperance movement in Wales. Entertainment of a trivial kind was provided by historical romances on subjects such as the life and loves of Dafydd ap Gwilym. Fiction was sometimes used as a medium for social criticism, as seen in the work of Samuel Roberts, or the exceptionally prolific Gwilym Hiraethog (William Rees, 1802–83), who adapted *Uncle Tom's Cabin* into Welsh, drawing attention to the evils of slavery, wrote a series of fictional letters in dialect on radical causes, 'Letters of the Old Farmer', and, in 1877, depicted the life of a farming community in *Helyntion Bywyd Hen Deiliwr* ('The Troubles of an Old Tailor's Life'). All these stories provide a necessary background to the work of Daniel Owen in the last quarter of the nineteenth century, who was the first Welsh author to realize fully the potential of the novel.

Daniel Owen (1836–95) was a native of Mold in Flintshire, close to the English border, and that small town provided the setting for all but one of his novels. He broke off his training for the ministry at Bala College to support his widowed mother and sister, working as a tailor and playing a prominent part in his Methodist chapel. His earliest attempts at fiction were based on incidents in the life of the chapel, and the religious perspective was essential to all his work. All his novels were first published in serial form in journals, a practice which exacerbated the rather aimless episodic construction which is the major weakness of his work. His great strengths are the creation of memorable characters, especially through lively dialogue, the revelation of their moral nature, often with devastating irony, and the depiction of social interaction against the background of a credible community.

His first major novel was *Rhys Lewis*, published in 1885. To tell the story of Rhys Lewis, minister of Bethel, Daniel Owen employed the fictional device of the autobiography (supposedly never intended for publication), drawing on the principal Welsh prose form of the period in order to convey the truth about his subject. It soon becomes apparent, however, that Rhys is unwilling to reveal the whole truth. A major theme of this and all Daniel Owen's work is hypocrisy, the gulf between man's social appearance and his inner nature. The novel can be divided into three distinct sections, each with quite different concerns. The first deals with the conflict between the traditional Calvinism of Rhys's mother Mari and the radical social ideals of his brother Bob, a coalminer who leads a strike for better conditions. The author's interest is in the moral problems which this radicalism poses for the chapel, and the unresolved conflict is eventually brought to an end by Bob's death in a pit accident. The second section is concerned with Rhys's spiritual development, and it is this which leads some critics to see the novel as Daniel Owen's profoundest work. The final section is the least satisfactory, involving the incredible complications and coincidences to which he resorted in place of a genuine plot.

Enoc Huws (1891) is set in the same community, but is less concerned with the affairs of the chapel. The eponymous hero is an illegitimate child, and the identity of his father is the central mystery of the story, but the novel is dominated by its anti-hero, Captain Trefor, a vividly realized rogue who deceives Enoc and others into investing money in his empty lead-mine. Enoc is in love with Captain Trefor's daughter Susi, and is narrowly saved from committing incest by the revelation at the end of the novel that Captain Trefor is in fact his father. Despite some looseness towards the end, *Enoc Huws* has a much tighter structure than *Rhys Lewis*, and the first eighteen chapters are a masterpiece of social comedy revealing the misunderstanding, self-deception, and hypocrisy which permeate human relationships. As in the story of Bob Lewis, a profound unease can be discerned here about the effects of industrial development on Welsh society.

With *Enoc Huws* Daniel Owen seems to have completed his

analysis of his own world, for in his last novel, *Gwen Tomos* (1894), he turned to the Flintshire countryside in the early part of the century, a period when Methodism was still a vital spiritual force on the fringes of society. The heroine seems to be based on the myth of Ann Griffiths, the passionate girl turned saint. The structure of the novel depends on contrasts and conflicts between religious and worldly characters, and as always it is obvious that Daniel Owen has a good deal of sympathy for the latter, particularly the spirited pagan Nansi'r Nant. A mystery as to parentage again provides the main story interest, the possibility being raised that Nansi is in fact

Daniel Owen

Captain Trefor

All of Wales has heard of the Pwllygwynt lead-mine. But perhaps not everyone knows that it was begun by Richard Trefor – that it was he who discovered the 'big lead'. From the first day that the discovery was made Richard Trefor's promotion was clear to everyone. He was no longer Richard Trefor, but Captain Trefor, if you please. Captain Trefor came to be looked upon as some Joseph sent by providence to keep many people alive. A sudden change took place in people's ideas about him. Those who used to frown upon him soon realized that that was just narrowmindedness on their part, and they lost no time in readjusting their opinion of him. What were formerly called sins in Richard were now merely weaknesses in Captain Trefor. Everyone had their faults, and even Captain Trefor could not be expected to be perfect. Captain Trefor's weaknesses were only natural, easily explained by now, and easily excused in a man *in his position*. Captain Trefor was a much better man than had previously been thought, and he was certainly a blessing to the neighbourhood. In a word, Captain Trefor was a good example of human nature's tendency to form a false opinion of a man when he is poor, and of how impossible it is for a man to be properly appreciated until he has achieved some degree of worldly success.

(Translated from Daniel Owen's novel *Enoc Huws*)

Gwen's mother, which would have interesting implications for the heroine's moral nature. Critics are divided as to which of these three novels is Daniel Owen's best work. All three have their particular qualities and strengths, and it must be accepted that throughout his short career the novelist was developing tentatively without ever fully realizing his talents in any one outstanding work. Nevertheless, he set a high standard for Welsh novelists of the twentieth century in many ways, above all in terms of the moral responsibility of the author to reveal the truth about his society.

8 The Literary Revival of the Early Twentieth Century

The literary revival which began in the last two decades of the nineteenth century was both a culmination of the development of Victorian Wales and also a reaction against essential aspects of Victorian culture. The new movement embodied the Liberal ideal of the devout and cultured common people encapsulated in the Welsh word *gwerin*. Most of its authors were products of the newly established education system, the county schools and the colleges of the University of Wales. For the first time Welsh language and literature became subjects of professional academic study, providing twentieth-century authors with a much firmer grasp of their literary inheritance. The optimism of the late Victorian period is clearly reflected in the new literature, based ultimately on the economic prosperity of Britain, to which Welsh industries contributed substantially, and on the belief in progress. At the turn of the century the future seemed to promise great things for Wales as her *gwerin* came into their own. Even the Welsh language was on the increase as a result of industrial development. However, the new movement also constituted a rejection of Victorian materialism. As the detrimental effects of industry became apparent authors tended to turn, like their counterparts such as Ruskin and William Morris in England, either to a pre-industrial and pre-colonial past in the myths of the Middle Ages, or else to a pastoral idyll in rural Wales, giving the movement a markedly Romantic character. There was widespread rebellion against the narrow puritanism of chapel religion and the pietism which dominated nineteenth-century literature. Welsh nationalism became more aggressively separatist, in contrast to the pride in plucky little Wales's contribution to the British Empire which was characteristic of Victorian patriotism.

The element of continuity in the revival is most obvious in the work of O. M. Edwards (1858–1920), a prolific author and editor who has had a formative influence on modern Welsh culture. His background and career epitomize the ideal of the *gwerin*. He came from humble origins in Llanuwchllyn to become a Fellow of Lincoln College, Oxford, and subsequently devoted his life to the promotion of the folk-culture of Wales, especially through the popular magazine *Cymru* ('Wales') which he edited from 1891 until his death. His own writing is primarily journalistic, travel books and essays in a light and readable style which sought to open the eyes of the Welsh people to the beauties of their own country and its past. His most important work is *Cartrefi Cymru* ('The Homes of Wales'), published in 1896, a collection of essays on his visits to the homes of important figures in Welsh cultural history such as Williams Pantycelyn and Ellis Wynne, combining history, literature and love of nature in an attempt to create a sense of sacred places.

The element of reaction in the revival is first seen in the work of Emrys ap Iwan (Robert Ambrose Jones, 1848–1906), a scathing critic of the sectarianism and Anglophilia of Victorian Wales. Whereas O. M. Edwards was immediately popular because his work embodied some of the most cherished ideals of the day, Emrys ap Iwan made himself unpopular by his criticism, and his importance was not fully appreciated until after his death. He is one of the fathers of modern Welsh nationalism and the language movement, ahead of his time in his recognition that language is not merely incidental, but is an essential aspect both of the mentality of a people and of their nationhood. He developed a lucid and rational prose style as a polemical weapon (influenced by the French essayists), and although he was not primarily a creative writer his satirical pieces are highly inventive. Emrys ap Iwan made an important contribution to the literary revival by drawing attention to the existence of a tradition of Welsh prose classics going back to the Bible, restoring standards which had been lost due to over-dependence on English models.

The leading scholar and literary critic in the new movement was John Morris-Jones (1864–1929). Together with O. M. Edwards, he was one of the founder members of the influential Oxford Welsh Society, *Cymdeithas Dafydd ap Gwilym*, in 1886. As professor of Welsh at the University College of North Wales, Bangor, he was the first to undertake a scientific study of the language and its literature. He set about purifying the written language of its recent corruptions, basing his reforms on the study of classical texts and on respect for natural spoken Welsh. His *Welsh Grammar* of 1913 is a definitive description of the literary language. As a critic, his main work was an equally definitive account of traditional Welsh poetics, *Cerdd Dafod* (1925), and his regular adjudications helped to raise the standards of eisteddfod competitions. The literary principles on which his criticism was based are a mixture of the Classical and the Romantic, combining emphasis on form and correct usage with the exaltation of feeling as the essential matter of poetry. His condemnations of didacticism and abstract thought in poetry are plainly too extreme, but at the time they were a necessary corrective to the metaphysical excesses of the New Poet. Similarly, his strictures on the use of everyday or debased language are relevant only to a narrow kind of lyric poetry, but were valuable in restoring awareness of the impact of words, which is one of the great strengths of the new movement. He exemplified his principles in lyrics of refined feeling, published in *Caniadau* (1907), including translations of Heine and Omar Khayyám which did much to bring back sensuality to Welsh poetry.

Poetry

The origins of the new literary movement are not easy to date precisely, and the sensuous lyric poetry of Elfed (Howell Elvet Lewis, 1860–1953) can certainly be seen as one of its forerunners, as can the novels of Daniel Owen. However, two essential features which are hardly apparent in the work of those two authors are the rejection of the moral and cultural standards of the preceding age and the deliberate recovery of a classical tradition. Four outstanding poets of the early twentieth century who typify those tendencies in varying ways are T. Gwynn Jones, R. Williams Parry, W. J. Gruffydd, and T. H. Parry-Williams.

The phenomenally prolific author and scholar T. Gwynn Jones (1871–1949) was the son of a Denbighshire crofter, from whom he learnt the art of *cynghanedd* in which he was to excel. With little formal education, he became a journalist, but his study of medieval Welsh poetry gained him a post as lecturer, and subsequently professor, in the Welsh department at Aberystwyth. T. Gwynn Jones was a versatile and restlessly energetic writer, producing several novels, plays and collections of essays, but it was as a poet that he made his most important contribution to Welsh literature. The greatest master of the strict metres since the Middle Ages (although he has his equals amongst the present generation), he developed a more flexible form in his long poems by using *cynghanedd* in a variety of freer metres, thus providing a solution to the problem faced by Goronwy Owen in the eighteenth century. The first major landmark of the literary revival was T. Gwynn Jones's *awdl* 'Ymadawiad Arthur' ('The Departure of Arthur'), which won the Chair of the National Eisteddfod in 1902. The story of King Arthur's departure to Afallon is taken from Tennyson's *Morte d'Arthur*, but the interpretation reflects the spirit of national revival at the time. Arthur's promise to return to lead his people is cunningly self-fulfilling, since the poem itself exemplifies the awakening which he prophesies, and is a powerful expression of the optimism of the period.

Over the following quarter century T. Gwynn Jones went on to compose a series of long poems on the theme of the search for a lost paradise, all based on ancient Celtic legend, which he regarded as an embodiment of eternal verities. Over the years the optimism of the revival can be seen to give way to spiritual uncertainty and despair. In his poem on the story of Prince Madog, composed at one of Europe's darkest hours, in 1917, the famous seafarer turns his back on the internecine strife of medieval Gwynedd, setting sail in search of a better land to the west, but unlike the legend of the discovery of America popular in the eighteenth century, his ship sinks in the middle of the Atlantic, so that the fulfilment of the spiritual quest remains an enigmatic possibility. The existence of an earthly paradise is in no doubt in 'Anatiomaros' (1925), depicting the traditional rituals of a Celtic tribe in Gaul, and yet in 'Argoed', composed two years later, such a way of life is shown to be under terminal threat from Roman imperialism, which clearly corresponds to the English threat to the Welsh language. Rather than suffer the loss of their traditions the people of Argoed commit communal suicide by setting fire to their forest. Such a purist view of culture is exemplified by the majestic elegance of these poems' style, which stands in increasingly ironic contrast to the bleakness of the poet's vision, an affirmation of the traditional values of Welsh culture in the face of their threatened extinction. His vision of the modern world is at its most desolate in a series of free-verse poems which he published under a pseudonym in 1934 and 1935. These were collected in *Y Dwymyn* ('Fever') in 1944, including what is perhaps his greatest long poem, 'Cynddilig', a reworking of part of the Llywarch Hen cycle as an indictment of war.

Robert Williams Parry (1884–1956) was brought up in the busy slate-quarrying community of Tal-y-sarn in Caernarfonshire. However, in keeping with the Romantic impulse of the period, he had a strong aesthetic aversion to his industrial environment, preferring to find his inspiration in the timeless landscape of the surrounding mountains or the nearby agricultural region of Eifionydd. He first came to prominence by winning the National Eisteddfod Chair in 1910 with his immensely popular *awdl* 'Yr Haf' ('Summer'), a melodious and hedonistic celebration of the joys of love and nature, darkened only by the agnostic's anxiety in the face

T. Gwynn Jones

from 'The Departure of Arthur'

'Over the waves there's a gracious country,
Nor in that land lingers lamentation;
Whoever comes there, no old age or pestilence
Strikes down, for the clean breeze of freedom
Keeps every heart of us nimble and merry,
As the Isle of Afallon itself is so.

'Old dreams are in that country of blessedness
That have eased the terror of countless ages;
All ancient hopes are alive for ever;
In that spot high purposes make progress;
No loss of faith comes there to scorch it,
Neither time of shame, nor breaking heart.

'There's fire in every singing inspiration!
Strength, confidence, relish to every endeavour!
Energy for those who'd change things the better,
And a basis always for wanting to hope!
We do not grow old while that protects us – right custom
It is, breath of life to the nation.'

(Translated by Tony Conran, *Welsh Verse*)

of transience. With hindsight the poem seems a poignant evocation of the carefree mood of the years immediately preceding the Great War. Williams Parry was long known as 'The Poet of Summer', although in fact he soon rejected such escapist Romanticism as he came to terms with the harsh reality of the war. His elegies to young men killed in the trenches have come to represent the sense of loss felt for a whole generation. Outstanding among these is the series of *englynion* for Hedd Wyn (Ellis H. Evans, 1887–1917), the poet from Trawsfynydd who was awarded the National Eisteddfod Chair a month after he was killed in action, and whose consequent mythic status is similar to that of Rupert Brooke in English. Williams Parry

T. H. Parry-Williams.

adhered to John Morris-Jones's principle of keeping propaganda out of literature, and his greatest strength as a poet is the tersely evocative handling of words to convey the intensity of his experience, as seen in one of the most popular nature poems in Welsh, the sonnet 'Y Llwynog' ('The Fox'). His poetic career divides quite neatly into two periods represented by his two published collections: *Yr Haf a Cherddi Eraill* ('Summer and Other Poems') of 1924, and *Cerddi'r Gaeaf* ('The Poems of Winter') of 1952. The finest poems in the later volume are those inspired by the burning of the Bombing School in 1936, as will be seen in the following chapter.

Another prodigiously energetic writer was W. J. Gruffydd (1881–1954), who played a central role in Welsh literary life throughout the first half of the twentieth century. As a scholar and critic he produced influential anthologies and studies, reinforcing John Morris-Jones's bias towards lyric poetry, and as editor of the leading literary journal, *Y Llenor*, he was an often scathing commentator on Welsh affairs. W. J. Gruffydd could be a moody and inconsistent man, and his poetry reflects the tensions in his personality, ranging from opulent Romanticism to stark realism. The ostentatious sensuality of his early work exemplifies the element of rebellion in the revival (he lost the Eisteddfod Crown in 1902 for his immoral interpretation of the Tristan and Isolde story), and yet he was very much a product of the Nonconformist culture of the nineteenth century. Strongly influenced by both O. M. Edwards and the novels of Thomas Hardy, he wrote a number of poems in a movingly plain style celebrating the stoical virtues of the common people of his native Caernarfonshire, which represent his most important contribution to Welsh literature.

Although T. H. Parry-Williams (1887–1975) was a product of the same literary movement as his older cousin Robert Williams Parry, his work represents a move away from the Romantic lyricism of the John Morris-Jones school, introducing a new realism and a more natural style. A brilliant academic career in several European universities led to a professorship in the Welsh Department at Aberystwyth, but his native village of Rhyd-ddu in Snowdonia remained his emotional anchor, and the bonds of attachment felt by the exile were a central theme of his writing. He achieved a remarkable double by winning both Chair and Crown at the National Eisteddfod in 1912 and again in 1915, shocking the judges by his realistic portrayal of the amoral life of Paris. His first volume of poetry, published in 1931, contains a number of finely wrought sonnets, but its most radical element is the group of poems in deceptively simple rhyming couplets using colloquial language to explore the paradoxes of human existence. His work has some modernist features, the loss of the old certainties, an awareness of life's complexity and relativity, the impression of a divided consciousness, and yet his self-deprecating irony continually undercuts the darkest visions of existential chaos. In parallel to his poetry he made extensive use of the literary essay as a medium for philosophical contemplation of a highly personal kind, revealing a sensitive and complex personality. Detachment was for him a distinctive attitude, a scientific frame of mind reinforced by a year spent studying medicine, but he was constantly aware of the irrational power of the emotions, and the tension between the two is essential to his work, as seen in his most famous poem, 'Hon' (literally 'This One', i.e. Wales), which has become a classic expression of the ambiguous loyalties of many Welsh people.

T. H. Parry-Williams was a conscientious objector during the First World War, and the disillusionment which he suffered then was clearly a factor in his development as a modernist poet. The war had a traumatic impact on Welsh culture, shattering the complacent certainties of the Victorian era and producing a harsher realism in literature. One of the few Welsh poets who could draw on personal experience of the front line was Cynan (Albert Evans-Jones, 1895–1970). His long poem 'Mab y Bwthyn' ('Son of the Cottage'), written in 1921, contains disturbingly vivid descriptions of the war, and yet in its sentimental account of the pure rural life it still belongs to the world of the Victorian lyric. Cynan subsequently backed away from the realism to which his war experiences had led him, and became a pillar of the Eisteddfod establishment, delighting in the popular appeal of its pageantry.

Drama

Welsh drama was very slow to develop, partly because of the lack of cities to support theatres in Wales. After the suppression of the folk-theatre of the interludes, Nonconformist disapproval effectively prevented the development of secular drama in the Victorian period, but towards the end of the nineteenth century a romantic nationalist theatre did flourish, producing historical pageants by authors such as Beriah Gwynfe Evans. It was not until just before the First World War that a dramatic movement emerged, in both English and Welsh, which dealt with contemporary Welsh society, following the example of the great Norwegian dramatist, Henrik Ibsen. This drama was the most public manifestation of the literary revival, and it also presented the most vigorous challenge to the Nonconformist Liberal establishment. Particularly outspoken in its criticism was W. J. Gruffydd's play, *Beddau'r Proffwydi* ('The Graves of the

T. H. Parry-Williams
'This Spot'

Why should I give a hang about Wales? It's by a mere fluke of
    fate
That I live in its patch. On a map it does not rate

Higher than a scrap of earth in a back corner,
And a bit of a bother to those who believe in order.

And who is it lives in this spot, tell me that.
Who but the dregs of society? Please, cut it out,

This endless chatter of oneness and country and race:
You can get plenty of these, without Wales, any place.

I've long since had it with listening to the croon
Of the Cymry, indeed, forever moaning their tune.

I'll take a trip, to be rid of their wordplay with tongue and
    with pen,
Back to where I once lived, aboard my fantasy's train.

And here I am then. Thanks be for the loss,
Far from all the fanatic's talkative fuss.

Here's Snowdon and its crew; here's the land, bleak and bare;
Here's the lake and river and crag, and look, over there,

The house where I was born. But see, between the earth and
    the heavens,
All through the place there are voices and apparitions.

I begin to totter somewhat, and I confess,
There comes over me, so it seems, a sort of faintness;

And I feel the claws of Wales tear at my heart.
God help me, I can't get away from this spot.

(Translated by Joseph Clancy, *Twentieth Century Welsh Poems*)

A portrait of Caradoc Evans by Evan Walters.

Prophets'), exposing the hypocrisy of an oppressive chapel hierarchy, which caused a considerable stir when it was produced in March 1913. The two outstanding playwrights of the pre-war period were J. O. Francis in English, whose *Change* (1912) deals with the strife caused by labour activism, and D. T. Davies in Welsh, whose dialect play *Ble ma fa?* ('Where is he?') of 1913 is a humanist critique of the Calvinist doctrine of salvation by faith. A striking feature of this drama movement is its bilingual nature, with English and Welsh sharing common themes and plays often being translated between the two languages. The two literatures of Wales have never enjoyed such a harmonious relationship since then, and it is a pity that it was Caradoc Evans rather than J. O. Francis who was to become the guiding spirit of Anglo-Welsh literature.

The beginnings of Anglo-Welsh literature

As already seen, Welsh writing in English has a long history, beginning with the English *englynion* to the Virgin Mary by the fifteenth-century bard Ieuan ap Hywel Swrdwal, composed to demonstrate the glories of Welsh poetics, and including notable poets in the early modern period such as Henry Vaughan and John Dyer. However, it is debatable whether such writers belong to a recognizably Anglo-Welsh literature, as opposed to English literature in general. Interesting borderline cases who have been claimed as Anglo-Welsh, although their Welshness is tenuous, are the Georgian lyricist W. H. Davies of Newport and Edward Thomas, who has perhaps become Anglo-Welsh in retrospect in view of his influence on later poets such as Alun Lewis and R. S. Thomas. Caradoc Evans is generally regarded as the founding father of modern Anglo-Welsh literature, in the sense of English-language writing with specifically Welsh concerns, but it was not until the 1930s that an Anglo-Welsh literary movement came into being, as a result of the social changes outlined in the next chapter. The term 'Anglo-Welsh' should not be taken to imply any dilution of Welshness; indeed, it is most fittingly used of those writers who assert their Welsh viewpoint most vigorously.

Caradoc Evans (1878–1945) achieved instant notoriety in 1915 with the publication of his first collection of short stories, *My People*, depicting the life of Manteg, an imaginary community based on the Cardiganshire village of Rhydlewis where Evans was brought up in poverty by his widowed mother. At the time Evans was working as a journalist in London, and it can be maintained that he wrote for an English audience, although he himself envisaged his role as that of an Old Testament prophet denouncing the sins of his people. His work was very well received in England, but its savage portrayal of a brutish and evil peasantry infuriated Welsh readers, leading to calls for the book to be banned. The stories are written in a unique and often grotesque style which is a blend of Biblical language and distorted translations from the

Welsh, but nevertheless has an intense hypnotic power. The basic impulse of Caradoc Evans's work was similar to that of other writers of the revival in its attack on the Nonconformist establishment, but he went much further than others in demolishing the cherished Liberal ideal of the devout and high-minded *gwerin*. His indignation at the exploitation of the peasantry by wealthy farmers and tradesmen indicates his socialist viewpoint, and his work is also an indictment of the oppression of women in a

Caradoc Evans
from 'A Father in Sion'

At the time of her marriage Achsah was ten years older than her husband. She was rich, too: Danyrefail, with its stock of good cattle and a hundred acres of fair land, was her gift to the bridegroom. Six months after the wedding Sadrach the Small was born. Tongues wagged that the boy was a child of sin. Sadrach answered neither yea nor nay. He answered neither yea nor nay until the first Communion Sabbath, when he seized the bread and wine from Old Shemmi and walked to the Big Seat. He stood under the pulpit, the fringe of the minister's Bible-marker curling on the bald patch on his head.

'Dear people', he proclaimed, the silver-plated wine cup in one hand, the bread plate in the other, 'it has been said to me that some of you think Sadrach the Small was born out of sin. You do not speak truly. Achsah, dear me, was frightened by the old bull. The bull I bought in the September fair. You, Shemmi, you know the animal. The red-and-white bull. Well, well, dear people, Achsah was shocked by him. She was running away from him, and as she crossed the threshold of Danyrefail, did she not give birth to Sadrach the Small? Do you believe me now, dear people. As the Lord liveth, this is the truth. Achsah, Achsah, stand you up now, and say you to the congregation if this is not right.'

Achsah, the babe suckling at her breast, rose and murmured:

'Sadrach speaks the truth.'

Sadrach ate of the bread and drank of the wine.

patriarchal society, although the unremittingly grim satire precludes sympathy for any of the characters. Caradoc Evans went on to produce a number of other works of fiction in the same vein, including a satirical portrait of the London Welsh, but he never matched the virulent intensity of his first book. His influence on the following generation of Anglo-Welsh writers was substantial, and led to a polarization of the two literatures of Wales, English becoming associated with hostility towards the Welsh language and the Liberal Nonconformist culture which it embodied.

9 The Inter-War Years

Ideologies

The literature of the period between the two world wars was coloured by the clash between conflicting political ideologies in many countries, and the shift towards politically committed writing affected most authors in one way or another. In Wales the dominant political conflict was that between nationalism and socialism, each offering different solutions to the economic crisis and consequent mass unemployment which afflicted the industrial valleys of the south in particular. The nationalist ideal was an independent Welsh nation with a primarily rural economy, which would involve the deindustrialization of the valleys, whilst the socialists were committed to the international struggle against capitalism in an effort to establish workers' control of industry. The nationalists regarded the Welsh language and its Christian culture as essential to the nation, whilst socialism at that time was a materialistic doctrine which saw Welsh culture as an anachronism and Christianity as a reactionary force. Due partly to the legacy of Caradoc Evans, and also to the dominance of socialism in the industrial areas where the Welsh language was in rapid decline, the two literatures tended to be polarized in their political allegiances. However, Welsh authors were by no means unanimous in their commitment to nationalism. There were those who adhered to the old Liberal ideals, such as W. J. Gruffydd and the poet Iorwerth Peate, founder of the Welsh Folk Museum, and others who held left-wing views, such as the admirably dedicated Communist poet T. E. Nicholas (Niclas y Glais, 1878–1971), and the younger Alun Llywelyn-Williams of Cardiff, whose first language was English. Nor were Anglo-Welsh writers invariably hostile to the Welsh language, as will be seen.

The predominance of the nationalist viewpoint in Welsh literature since the 1930s is largely due to the enormous influence of one man, Saunders Lewis, who was one of the founders of the Welsh Nationalist Party (later Plaid Cymru) in 1925. And the decisive event which galvanized many Welsh writers into political commitment was the burning of the RAF bombing school at

Penyberth in the Welsh heartland of the Llŷn peninsula in 1936 by Saunders Lewis and two colleagues, the author D. J. Williams and the Baptist minister Lewis Valentine. Peaceful protests against the establishment of the bombing school having failed, the action was taken in order to publicize the issue, giving Lewis the opportunity to make a court speech on the primacy of the moral law over the law of the state. A guilty verdict was only achieved after the case had been transferred from Caernarfon to the Old Bailey, and as a result of his nine-month prison sentence Saunders Lewis was sacked from his post in the Welsh Department at University College, Swansea. The affair had a particularly dramatic effect on the poetic career of R. Williams Parry, inspiring him to break his self-imposed silence with a series of caustic sonnets expressing his scorn for the moral cowardice of the Welsh people, all the more virulent because he included himself in that judgement.

John Saunders Lewis
Saunders Lewis (1893–1985) was brought up in a Welsh-speaking family in Liverpool, a fact which may partly explain his detached

Lewis Valentine, Saunders Lewis and D. J. Williams on their way to Pwllheli Magistrates' Court in September 1936. Photograph taken by J. E. Jones.

R. Williams Parry

'J. S. L.'

You stooped from your heaven to the grains on the cosy yard
Blinding with your colour all the chicks and the pullets;
And created in the dove-cote doors above your head
The old, old flutter that occurs among doves.
You were a fool, O forsaken one, a fool; for woe
To a bird without kin and a peerless soul without backing;
Without descent from the same homestead in the same field's
    corner –
Without a body of like clay or a god of the same substance.
And we continue to drink sagely, sometimes tea
And sometimes learning in our chambers' afternoon peace;
And on our classical hearing and the spirit of the place
The noise of the parish pump or the cells' iron gates never
    breaks.
Prudently we eat, slice after four-sided slice,
The academic toast. As for you, enjoy the gruel.

(Translated by Joseph Clancy, *Twentieth Century Welsh Poems*)

conception of Wales as a whole rather than the identification with a particular region which is typical of most modern authors. His commitment to his country was an act of will, inspired by his reading of French nationalist thinkers during the First World War, and his life and work were based on a coherent philosophy of moral responsibility. Although belonging to a prominent Methodist family, he converted to Catholicism in 1932, in accordance with his belief in the value of the Catholic faith and culture in uniting the countries of medieval Europe without threatening their political independence. His social ideals were highly conservative, emphasizing patriarchal order, the paternalistic role of the aristocracy, and the importance of tradition in transmitting moral and cultural values through the essential unit of the family. These ideals were set out in political essays he wrote on behalf of Plaid Cymru, and exemplified in his creative writing. As a literary critic he revealed (some would say created) the significance of the literary tradition as an essential component of Welsh nationhood, in much the same way as T. S. Eliot did for the English tradition. He laid particular stress on the classical poetry of the Catholic Middle Ages as the mirror of an ideal social order at a time when Wales participated in the culture of Europe rather than being an adjunct to England.

Saunders Lewis's main creative medium was the drama, the form most suited to his belief in the individual's obligation to take action in defence of his or her moral principles. However, he also published two novels, *Monica* (1930), discussed below, and *Merch Gwern Hywel* (1964), and a small but wide-ranging body of poetry which contains astringent comment on the state of Wales as well as some of the finest religious poems of modern times. His skill as a poet was of course an essential factor in his success as a playwright, and verse dramas such as *Buchedd Garmon* and *Blodeuwedd* contain some of his most powerful passages of poetry. His dramatic career spanned over fifty years, beginning, interestingly enough, with a play in English, *The Eve of Saint John* (1921). His first major work was *Buchedd Garmon* ('The Life of Garmon') in 1937, an inspiring account of the defence of Christian civilization in Wales against the barbarian threat, clearly reflecting the stand which he himself had taken in the previous year.

The beginning of Lewis's most productive period as a dramatist was marked by the completion of *Blodeuwedd* in 1948, a play left unfinished since the 1920s, when it represented a moral challenge to the dominant Romanticism of the period. Based on the story of Lleu's unfaithful wife from the fourth branch of the *Mabinogi* (see chapter 3), it exemplifies Lewis's talent for drawing contemporary significance out of material from legend and history, demonstrating the importance of cultural tradition through the tragedy of Blodeuwedd's rootless condition. The marital relationship is further explored in *Siwan* (1954), a story from medieval history in which Llywelyn the Great's Anglo-Norman wife is caught in adultery. Llywelyn's vengeful execution of the lover leads to complete emotional estrangement between husband and wife, but the play's final act is a marvellously sensitive enactment of the restoration of mutual understanding and forgiveness. As in all Lewis's work, marital harmony is shown to be the essential basis of the well-being of the whole society, and the patriarchal theory leaves the wife very much subordinate to the husband's public role, although she is in fact depicted as the more perceptive of the two.

Two plays with a contemporary European setting which deal with the moral problems arising from the political tensions of the Cold War period are *Gymerwch Chi Sigaret?* ('Will You Have a Cigarette?') and *Brad* ('Treason'), published in 1955 and 1958 respectively, both dominated by the threat which Communism posed to Christian Europe. Lewis's Catholic faith is most vigorously asserted in *Gymerwch Chi Sigaret?*, in which the wife plays a guiding role similar to that of Dante's Beatrice.

All these works present heroes and heroines fulfilling their moral

Saunders Lewis

Emrys asks Bishop Garmon to accompany him to battle

A man planted a vineyard on a fruitful hillside,
He dug and planted in it the best vines,
He built a wall around it and raised a tower in the centre,
And gave it to his son as an inheritance
To preserve his name from generation to generation.
But a herd of pigs broke down the wall of the vineyard
And rushed in to trample and graze;
Is it not right that the son should stand in the breach now
And call his companions to him,
So that the gap be mended and his inheritance saved?
Garmon, Garmon,
My country of Wales is a vineyard given into my keeping,
To be passed on to my children
And to my children's children
As an inheritance for all time;
And lo, the pigs are rushing to despoil it.
So I call now upon my companions,
The common man and the scholar,
Come to me in the breach,
Stand with me in the gap,
That the beauty of the past be preserved for the ages to come.

(Translated from *Buchedd Garmon* ('The Life of Garmon'))

obligation to act rationally in accordance with their beliefs, and hold out at least some hope that such action is worthwhile. By the sixties, however, Lewis's vision was becoming increasingly pessimistic, as seen in the most powerful of his later plays, *Cymru Fydd* ('The Wales of the Future'), published in 1967, in which the cynical actions of the anti-hero are an expression of his disillusionment at the moral degeneration of his country. Hope is nevertheless held out by the possibility that his idealistic girlfriend may be pregnant, representing the beginnings of Welsh-language protest movements partially inspired by Lewis's radio lecture of 1962, *Tynged yr Iaith* ('The Fate of the Language'). Saunders Lewis's literary stature is difficult to separate from his enormous political influence, but his particular contribution to Welsh literature involved the restoration of a sense of the past and a European dimension, a renewed awareness of man's sinful nature, and perhaps above all an interest in ideas exemplified in action.

The rural ideal

The Welsh Nationalist ideal of the organic rural community is reflected in a good deal of the literature of this period. The ideal was of course valid for the whole of rural Wales, but it became epitomized in literature by the village of Rhydcymerau in north Carmarthenshire because two leading Welsh writers happened to have their origins there, D. J. Williams and Gwenallt. The short-story writer D. J. Williams (1885–1970) has given an account of his upbringing at Rhydcymerau in the first volume of his autobiography. *Hen Dŷ Ffarm* ('The Old Farmhouse'), published in 1953, is a classic description of a close-knit farming community which draws heavily on the oral tradition in style and structure. It was D. J. Williams who popularized the expression *milltir sgwâr* (square mile) for the place of one's roots, with its suggestion of wholeness and harmony. His short stories, published in 1936, 1941 and 1949, form a trilogy entitled *Storïau'r Tir* ('Stories of the Land'), and their development reflects the decline of the rural way of life during the author's lifetime, from the self-contained world of the early stories to the disintegration under pressures from outside. D. J. Williams was an accomplished satirist, and as a pacifist and Christian nationalist he wrote scathingly of the militaristic jingoism of two world wars.

The poet David James Jones (Gwenallt, 1899–1968) belonged to Rhydcymerau at one remove, his parents having come from there to the industrial Swansea Valley. A committed socialist in his youth,

D. J. Williams
John Jenkins the dealer

And after reaching our kitchen of a Saturday night, when two packed pipes were drawing in consolation for my father and for him and another mile was in store for him before setting eyes again on his cheerful but penetrating Chancellor, John Jenkins now had just what he wanted, the opportunity to review the week's journey. It is true that such ordinary things as market prices and weather forecasts of heat or rain or dry wind, with an estimate of its probable effect on the season's condition would come in incidentally. But such was never the main course of the conversation. Had it been so John Jenkins would hardly have set foot in my story up to this time. But places and persons and incidents, stories about people and their sayings, it was these things that chiefly claimed his advertence. John Jenkins was a man who lived in a closely woven society, and that warmth was enough to keep him snug and happy throughout his life.

In recounting a fair or a market he did not deem it sufficient to mention this or that person whom he had met there and the talk they had had together. He had to go into details about him at once, connecting him with some family or kindred known to all the company. And often, in order to complete his index card, a step or two was taken on the track of his wife's relatives, and they too were brought in. Often the marginal notes were the most interesting part. I know of no plain countryman making a continent so rich in interest of his own county as this contented old dealer. John Jenkins was born in the late thirties of the last century. For everything except the trivialities of business his observation was intent and his memory tenacious. He remembered accounts he had heard of events in the neighbourhood long before his birth. Listening to him all the evening as I did time and time again, one got a wonderful saga of the characters and folklife of Carmarthenshire and its borders throughout almost the whole of the last century.

(From *Hen Dŷ Ffarm*, translated by Waldo Williams)

he was imprisoned during the First World War for refusing to fight for British imperialism, but under the influence of the new Welsh Nationalist Party he reverted to his Christian inheritance and came to uphold the rural community of his family origins as the solution to the crisis facing industrial Wales. Gwenallt's poetry speaks for generations of Welsh people in the industrial areas who felt their roots to be in the countryside, and yet he himself stood detached from both worlds as a lecturer in Welsh at the University College of Wales in Aberystwyth. He sought a synthesis of the two, continuing to value socialism's concern for justice (see below on his treatment of his industrial background), and yet the balance was tilted very much in favour of the rural on ideological grounds. Some of his most powerful poems deal with man's sinful nature, which in his view undermined socialist idealism, and he saw the Depression as primarily a spiritual crisis rather than a merely economic one. Gwenallt published five volumes of poetry, the two most important being his first, *Ysgubau'r Awen* ('Sheaves of the Muse'), in 1939, and his third, *Eples* ('Leaven') in 1951. His direct and raw style had a striking impact after the refined lyricism of Welsh poetry in the previous generation, and his work combines harsh realism with visionary idealism. One of his best-known poems is 'Rhydcymerau', in protest against the destruction by afforestation of the community which embodied his social ideal.

The nationalist rural ideal applied primarily to the Welsh-speaking areas of west Wales. The border country of the east produced a less ideologically committed literature, using the English language of necessity and reflecting profoundly divided allegiances, but nevertheless evincing the same concern for the decline of rural communities. The foremost writer of this region is Geraint Goodwin (1903–41) from Newtown, a Fleet Street journalist whose promising literary career was tragically cut short by his early death from tuberculosis. Goodwin is best known for his first novel, *The Heyday in the Blood* (1936), an evocative depiction of the traditional life of a Welsh border village under threat from the modern world. In addition to two other novels he published a fine collection of short stories, *The White Farm* (1937). There is a romanticizing tendency in his treatment of the contrast between the superficial Anglicized culture of the town and the profound Welsh heritage of the countryside. Another important border writer is Peggy Whistler (1909–58), who published novels and short stories under the pen-name Margiad Evans (the surname of Welsh ancestors). Much of her youth was spent in the border country of Herefordshire, and she felt an imaginative affinity with Wales. She published four novels in the 1930s, conceiving of the border as a location of conflict, but her finest work is in the short stories collected in *The Old and the Young* (1948), which contain vivid evocations of sensual experiences.

The divided allegiances of the border region are also significant as background to the work of the playwright Emlyn Williams (b. 1905), who has had considerable success on the English stage. His best-known play, *The Corn is Green* (1938), shows academic success alienating a young man from his rural Welsh community, based on Williams's own Flintshire village. His work combines realism with lyrical power, but is sometimes marred by sentimentality and a tendency towards melodrama. A more complex treatment of the theme of alienation through education is found in the novels of Raymond Williams, discussed in the next chapter.

The literature of industrial south Wales
The first flowering of Welsh writing in English took place in the 1930s as an inevitable result of the increasing dominance of the English language in south-east Wales. Some of the authors were from Welsh-speaking families, but they had little formal education in Welsh and tended to associate the language with the repressive puritanism of the chapels. Conceptions of audience oscillated between south Wales and London, where publishers were based, but in either case English was the common language. The first recognizable group of authors who can be termed Anglo-Welsh (following the example of social criticism set by Caradoc Evans and J. O. Francis) were the novelists who responded to the economic crisis by depicting the sufferings and struggles of valleys communities. The very subject matter gave their work a radical impact, exposing social injustice in one of the most deprived areas in Britain, and several of the authors did share the left-wing commitment which was dominant in English writing in the thirties, but as a whole the literature displays a wide spectrum of political viewpoints. One of its most valuable aspects is that most of the authors had personal experience of the working-class life which they depicted, in contrast to the middle-class intellectuals of the Auden circle.

Pioneering depictions of valleys life occur in the work of Joseph Keating (1871–1934), but the first industrial novel of the Depression period was *Rhondda Roundabout* of 1934 by Jack Jones (1884–1970), a coalminer's son from Merthyr Tydfil. As its title suggests, it is a lively and colourful spectacle of the variety of Rhondda life, holding the conflicting elements in balance. A number of other novels by Jack Jones trace the development of industrial south Wales over several generations with great narrative vigour. Gwyn Jones's novel of 1936, *Times Like These*, is a much more subdued treatment of the drab life of a working-class family blighted by the 1926 strike. Born in Blackwood, Monmouthshire, in 1907, Gwyn Jones has had a distinguished academic career (including his outstanding translation of the *Mabinogion* in collaboration with Thomas Jones), and his fiction and editorial work have made him a major figure in Anglo-Welsh literature for over fifty years.

Overt political commitment first enters the Welsh industrial novel in the work of Lewis Jones (1897–1939), a coalminer and Communist activist from the Rhondda, who wrote two novels at the very end of his brief and busy life, *Cwmardy* (1937), and its sequel, *We Live* (1939). These portray the political development of a young miner, Len (based largely on the author's own experience), his growing awareness of injustice and the power of workers'

Gwyn Thomas.

unions, through the struggles of the 1930s, culminating in his martyrdom for the Republican cause in Spain. Lewis Jones's novels are remarkable for their treatment of women, with Len's wife Mary eschewing the conventional maternal role and playing an active part in politics. Although marred by melodrama and a sometimes stilted style, his work conveys a forceful sense of energy deriving from his conviction that the people have the power to shape their own future. A radical socialist viewpoint is also presented in the novels, short stories and plays of Gwyn Thomas (1913–81), a coalminer's son from the Rhondda who won a scholarship to Oxford, and became a teacher of modern languages. His first novel, *Sorrow For Thy Sons*, written in 1936, was rejected by Gollancz because its depiction of life on the dole was so unremittingly grim. Thomas subsequently developed a comic and absurdist mode which enabled him to approach the suffering of his people more indirectly, expressing his indignation with savage wit, best seen in *The Alone to the Alone* (1947). His most ambitious work is the unconventional historical novel *All Things Betray Thee* (1949), based on the Merthyr Rising of 1831 but dealing with the theme of the artist's role in the continuing working-class struggle. He subsequently pursued similar themes in his writing for the theatre, again dealing with the Merthyr Rising in the play *Jackie the Jumper* (1963). Gwyn Thomas was notorious for his derogatory remarks about the Welsh language, and after Caradoc Evans it is his work above all which epitomizes Anglo-Welsh antagonism towards the Nonconformist culture of rural Wales.

The tendency to process images of the Welsh valleys for consumption by English audiences is seen to some extent in the work of Rhys Davies, and was taken to extremes by Richard Llewellyn. Rhys Davies (1903–78) was the son of a Rhondda grocer who made a career as a professional writer in London, producing a prolific flow of novels and short stories on a wide variety of subjects, often drawing on his experience of industrial south Wales (seen from a distinctively *petit bourgeois* viewpoint), and also constructing fantasies of Welsh rural life, as in his best-known novel, *The Black Venus* (1944). Davies was fascinated by flamboyant characters who defy convention, and their sexuality figures prominently in his work. Richard Llewellyn (1906–83) was a much more orthodox writer who manipulated Welsh stereotypes with great skill to produce his phenomenal bestseller, *How Green Was My Valley* (1939), certainly the most famous novel about Wales. The inspired title conveys the novel's mythic theme, the

Idris Davies.

Eden of the early industrial community destroyed by exploitation and the encroachment of foreigners with their divisive socialism. Although *How Green Was My Valley* is a highly entertaining novel with considerable poetic force, its superficially innocuous pageantry in fact conceals a sinister form of nationalism which can justly be termed Fascist in view of its xenophobic stress on racial purity and its celebration of militaristic virtues.

The novel was certainly the most appropriate form for documentary accounts of proletarian life, but the poet Idris Davies (1905–53) managed to do something similar by breaking away from the conventional aesthetic concerns of poetry in order to deal with the ugliness of everyday life in a decaying industrial environment, following the lead of T. S. Eliot and the left-wing poets of the thirties. Davies had experience of work as a coalminer in the Rhymney Valley, but after the 1926 strike left him unemployed he managed to qualify as a teacher, spending most of his working life in London. He initially wrote poetry in Welsh, his first language, but rebellion against chapel religion combined with the inspirational influence of English poetry led him to choose English as his main medium. His work is uneven in quality, but at his best he conveys a powerful sense of indignation in scathing satires such as the poem quoted below. Idris Davies is a classic example of the uncertainty of voice which has been such a problem for Anglo-

Welsh poets, and his poetry often seems derivative, but he developed his own technique of ironic echo and contrast in order to exploit this very weakness, making effective use of the sequence form in his two major works, *Gwalia Deserta* of 1938, depicting effects of the Depression, and *The Angry Summer* of 1943, dealing with the miners' strike of 1926. The latter is his masterpiece, a poem of many voices which dramatizes the aspirations and tensions of that passionate struggle.

On the whole Welsh-language authors did not give a great deal of attention to the industrial south, and when they did their view tended to be a very negative one coloured by the rural ideal, especially in poetry. The most extreme condemnation is Saunders Lewis's notorious poem depicting the spiritual paralysis caused by

Idris Davies

Gwalia Deserta XXVI

The village of Fochriw grunts among the higher hills;
The dwellings of miners and pigeons and pigs
Cluster around the little grey war memorial.
The sun brings glitter to the long street roofs
And the crawling promontories of slag,
The sun makes the pitwheels to shine,
And praise be to the sun, the great unselfish sun,
The sun that shone on Plato's shoulders,
That dazzles with light the Taj Mahal.
The same sun shone on the first mineowner,
On the vigorous builder of this brown village,
And praise be to the impartial sun.
He had no hand in the bruising of valleys,
He had no line in the vigorous builder's plans,
He had no voice in the fixing of wages,
He was the blameless one.
And he smiles on the village this morning,
He smiles on the far-off grave of the vigorous builder,
On the ivied mansion of the first mineowner,
On the pigeon lofts and the Labour Exchange,
And he smiles as only the innocent can.

the Depression, 'Y Dilyw 1939' ('The Deluge 1939'), which says of the industrial wasteland of the Merthyr-Dowlais region, 'Here once was Wales'. Gwenallt's poetry shows more compassion for the sufferings of the proletariat, with a strong residue of the socialist anger of his youth, but he too tends to portray industrial workers in a very negative manner as a degenerate and subhuman mass, redeemed only by the chapel religion which enabled them to transcend their circumstances. The poet and dramatist J. Kitchener Davies (1902–52) of Cardiganshire could write with authority of the Rhondda Valley, having spent most of his working life there as a teacher and Plaid Cymru activist. His play *Cwm Glo* ('Coal Valley') caused controversy in 1935 by its frank treatment of immoral behaviour, representing the moral crisis facing industrial south Wales. In his most substantial work, the long poem of spiritual self-searching, *Sŵn y Gwynt sy'n Chwythu* ('The Sound of the Wind that Blows'), broadcast on radio a few days before the author's death in 1952, the Anglicized Rhondda is depicted as defenceless against the destructive wind, in contrast to his rural home with its sheltering hedges. The industrial south is the location of a few of Kate Roberts's short stories, which give a valuable view of the effects of poverty in the home, and a valleys community is depicted through north-Walian eyes in the novel *William Jones* (1944) by T. Rowland Hughes, but both authors were more at ease dealing with the slate-quarrying communities of their native Caernarfonshire.

Welsh fiction
The Welsh novel has developed by fits and starts during the twentieth century, without ever forming a sustained tradition. Daniel Owen's influence was enormous at the turn of the century, but no novelist came anywhere near his standard. Progress was made between the wars, with E. Tegla Davies's novel *Gŵr Pen y Bryn* ('The Master of Pen y Bryn'), in 1923, dealing with the radicalism of the nineteenth-century Tithe Wars and the difficult subject of spiritual conversion. Saunders Lewis's short novel *Monica* has been the subject of controversy ever since its publication in 1930, the main character being an amoral woman who uses her sexuality to dominate her husband. Set in Cardiff and Swansea, it is a virulent condemnation of rootless suburban life and the narcissism of sexual lust, similar in theme to Lewis's play *Blodeuwedd*.

Modern Welsh fiction is dominated by the short-story writer and

Kate Roberts.

novelist Kate Roberts (1891–1985) of Rhosgadfan in Caernarfonshire. Having studied under John Morris-Jones at Bangor she qualified as a teacher of Welsh, and her writing combines rich dialect with a classical literary style. Kate Roberts was the first Welsh writer to emulate the European masters in using the short story to explore characters' inner lives, without losing the compelling quality of the Welsh story's origins in oral tales. Her writing falls into two distinct periods, the first from 1925 to 1937, when she was living in south Wales and writing mainly about the struggle of working-class people against poverty, and the second from 1949 to 1981, by which time she had moved to the town of Denbigh in Clwyd. Her later work deals with the psychological problems of a more materially prosperous but fragmented society, which are very forcefully presented in her novella of 1962 about mental breakdown, *Tywyll Heno* ('Dark Tonight' – a quotation from the Heledd cycle, see chapter 2). The difference between the two periods should not be overestimated, however, since it is the emotional effects of hardship which concern her in her earlier work too, most notably in the superb collection of stories, *Ffair Gaeaf* ('Winter Fair') published in 1937. Humour is rare in Kate Roberts's writing, but a lighter side to her work is seen in the acutely observed stories about childhood in the 1959 collection *Te yn y Grug* ('Tea in the Heather').

The industrial novel begins in Welsh with Kate Roberts's classic *Traed mewn Cyffion* ('Feet in Chains') of 1936, a work of compressed brevity but epic spirit which depicts the history of a family spanning four generations, and through them the population movements which formed the industrial communities of Caernarfonshire, culminating in the cataclysm of the First World War. Kate Roberts has little to say about industrial work as such, since her focus is very much on the domestic sphere. The work of the quarry itself is dealt with more directly in the novels of T. Rowland Hughes (1903–49), a quarryman's son from Llanberis. His five novels were all written in the last years of his life when he was suffering from multiple sclerosis, and are based mainly on memories of life in the slate-quarrying communities of his youth. The finest is *Chwalfa* ('Dispersal'), published in 1946, an account of the hardship and social disruption caused by the lengthy strike in the Penrhyn quarries at the beginning of the century. Rowland Hughes is similar to Kate Roberts in portraying the stoical heroism of his people, but his view of life is a more optimistic one, and his characters conform much more to the ideal of the virtuous *gwerin*. That ideal is entirely shattered by the greatest in this series of Welsh slate-quarrying novels, Caradog Prichard's *Un Nos Ola Leuad* ('One Moonlit Night') of 1961, a harrowing depiction of a community in the process of disintegration, narrated with nightmarish clarity by a madman reliving his childhood.

Modernism

The modernist tendency in the literature of Wales had a variety of different aspects in the thirties and forties, and the writers gathered in this section were far from a homogeneous movement. What they have in common is the way in which their work challenged conventional modes of writing (and also of reading), making it the most imaginatively stimulating literature, and sometimes the most difficult, that Wales has produced. To some extent modernism constituted a reaction against the fashion for documentary realism and social commitment in the thirties, and involved an elaborate and highly personal poetic style which relied heavily on images and had a strong surrealist element, as seen especially in the work of Dylan Thomas. But on the other hand, modernist writing in both English and Welsh certainly conveyed a forceful impression of the anxious atmosphere of the years leading up to the Second World War. A characteristic of the English modernist movement was the widening of cultural context by allusion. This technique has been used extensively by some Anglo-Welsh authors, most notably the London Welshman David Jones (1895–1974), as a means of proclaiming their affinity and allegiance to the Welsh cultural inheritance which language-loss had partially denied them. David Jones's two long poems, *In Parenthesis* (1937), based on his experience as a private with the Royal Welsh Fusiliers during the First World War, and *The Anathémata* (1952), are densely textured celebrations of the cultural diversity of the Island of Britain which draw on a wide range of historical and mythic material in an attempt to restore lost continuities with the past.

Dylan Thomas (1914–53) is the most famous of all the poets of Wales, on account of his notorious lifestyle as much as the artistry and lyrical power of his poetry. Born in Swansea to Welsh-speaking parents from the west with middle-class aspirations, he was deprived of the Welsh language, but imbued by his father with a love of English poetry. Thomas's bohemianism was a rebellion against both his stifling suburban upbringing and repressive Welsh puritanism. He did, however, spend a good deal of time with country relatives as a boy, which was to prove a fruitful source of inspiration in his mature poetry. His attitude towards Wales was profoundly ambiguous, and he was drawn to the literary life of London in the thirties, but nevertheless Swansea and rural Carmarthenshire were crucial backgrounds to his writing, and it was his return to live in Wales towards the end of the war, eventually in the village of Laugharne, which inaugurated the most creative period of his life. Dylan Thomas's early poetry is preoccupied with adolescent sexuality and has an arresting but opaque style, as do the surrealistic short stories in the collection *The Map of Love* (1939). The bombing of London during the War inspired some of his most passionately felt poems, such as

The young Dylan Thomas.

'Ceremony after a Fire Raid', proclaiming the sanctity of life with extensive use of Christian mythology. The myth of Eden is particularly prominent in his later work, and lies at the heart of one of his finest poems, 'Fern Hill', in which boyhood visits to a family farm are exuberantly recreated with a keen sense of the loss inflicted by time. The intricate verbal texture of that poem is typical of Dylan Thomas's carefully crafted verse, and may well relate to Welsh poetic techniques. The comic realism of Dylan's later fiction parallels the development of his verse towards a greater objectivity and human sympathy, seen at its most genial in his 'play for voices', *Under Milk Wood* (published in 1954), a delightfully evocative celebration of life in the village of Llareggub, based mainly on Laugharne. Dylan's work was received with considerable acclaim during his lifetime, especially in America, and he had some success as a scriptwriter, but he never managed to benefit financially from his writing. His lifestyle took its final toll when he died of excessive drinking in New York in 1953.

Two writers closely associated with Dylan Thomas who have nevertheless made quite distinct contributions to the literature of Wales are Vernon Watkins and Glyn Jones. Like Thomas, the poet Vernon Watkins (1906–67) was deprived of the Welsh language by his parents. The two poets were friends and mutual critics, but in character Watkins was the complete opposite of Thomas, leading an introverted and orderly life working as a bank clerk in Swansea, although equally dedicated to the craft of poetry. Watkins was profoundly disturbed by life's transience, to the point of breakdown in his early twenties, and his poetry is a metaphysical search for an answer to the problem of time, in affirmation of an eternal order. He did move towards a Christian philosophy, but was also deeply attracted to the Welsh legend of the visionary poet Taliesin with its theme of regeneration. Vernon Watkins is one of the most demanding of Anglo-Welsh poets, but also among the most rewarding, as his elaborate but consistent symbolic system becomes clear, grounded in the landscape of his beloved Gower.

Glyn Jones was born in Merthyr Tydfil in 1905, and the vigorous life of that industrial town has been central to his writing, in balance with his family origins in the Carmarthenshire village of Llanstephan. Although Welsh was his first language, an Anglicized education and early admiration for English literature made it inevitable that English should be his creative medium. He does, however, have a thorough knowledge of Welsh culture, and has always promoted mutual understanding between the two literatures of Wales, as seen in his warmly sympathetic study, *The Dragon Has Two Tongues* (1968). His often-quoted statement on this matter is representative of Anglo-Welsh commitment to Wales, typically playing down the potential tension between medium and material:

> While using cheerfully enough the English language, I have never written in it a word about any country other than Wales, or any people other than Welsh people.

Glyn Jones has made a richly varied contribution to Anglo-Welsh literature for over fifty years, beginning with the publication of a collection of short stories, *The Blue Bed*, in 1937, followed by *Poems* in 1939. His novels came later, the finest being *The Island of Apples* (1965), a unique blend of imagination and observation, the Avalon of youthful fantasy set within the vividly real world of Merthyr.

Glyn Jones

'Remembering Mari'

Below the ward's darkening window
   I kiss the old inflamed cheek,
Hard, glassy, chill to my lips,
   And see a young woman at dusk walk
From the dark farmhouse, beside the hedge,
   While summer lightning flickers.
She crosses with the child the hill field's gloom,
   Between them the earthenware pitcher –
They bear now no thought, no knowledge,
   Of body's bliss, the agony, the squalor.
The stars burn low over the earth,
   We skirt the dark rick of kindling,
The pony's gold looms from the alders.
   Down at the sloping end of the grass
We reach the well's chill waters,
   We bury our cream under a dish of stars.
At the window the lightning's vein throbs agonised
   In the flesh of darkness, as I kiss, despairing,
For the last time, the crimson, stone-cold cheek.

Glyn Jones regards himself as a poet first and foremost, and all his work is suffused by his delight in verbal music and imagery, in which he draws inspiration from the medieval *cywyddwyr*. The visual quality which is so typical of Anglo-Welsh writing is nowhere

Alun Lewis

'In Hospital: Poona (1)'

Last night I did not fight for sleep
But lay awake from midnight while the world
Turned its slow features to the moving deep
Of darkness, till I knew that you were furled,

Beloved, in the same dark watch as I.
And sixty degrees of longitude beside
Vanished as though a swan in ecstasy
Had spanned the distance from your sleeping side.

And like to swan or moon the whole of Wales
Glided within the parish of my care:
I saw the green tide leap on Cardigan,
Your red yacht riding like a legend there,

And the great mountains, Dafydd and Llywelyn,
Plynlimmon, Cader Idris and Eryri
Threshing the darkness back from head and fin,
And also the small nameless mining valley

Whose slopes are scratched with streets and sprawling graves
Dark in the lap of firwoods and great boulders
Where you lay waiting, listening to the waves –
My hot hands touched your white despondent shoulders

– And then ten thousand miles of daylight grew
Between us, and I heard the wild daws crake
In India's starving throat; whereat I knew
That Time upon the heart can break
But love survives the venom of the snake.

stronger than in the work of Glyn Jones, reflecting his keen interest in painting. Although he has preferred the elemental lyricism of Dylan Thomas to the social conscience of Idris Davies, his work is full of human warmth and sympathy for people's idiosyncracies. His priorities are clear in his wonderfully witty poem, 'Merthyr' (the best introduction to his work), where he ultimately declares his allegiance to the people of his home town rather than the beauties of the surrounding hills.

Although most of the first wave of Anglo-Welsh writers were brought up in industrial Glamorgan, the countryside of south Carmarthenshire came to be a kind of surrogate heartland and source of inspiration for a number of them. Dylan Thomas's Fern Hill was located at Llan-gain, just a few miles from Glyn Jones's family home at Llanstephan. Dylan himself, of course, settled at Laugharne, where the novelist Richard Hughes, author of *High Wind in Jamaica* (1929) also made his home. The poet and editor Keidrych Rhys was from Llangadog, and lived during the war at Llan-y-bri with his wife Lynette Roberts, herself a poet of striking originality whose work records her painful experiences of civilian life in a west Wales village. Keidrych Rhys's most important contribution to Welsh writing in English was as editor of the magazine *Wales*, founded in 1937, which provided a valuable focus for the Anglo-Welsh poets and short-story writers discussed in this chapter.

Combatants' experience of the Second World War is expressed in the work of Alun Lewis in English and Alun Llywelyn-Williams in Welsh, although neither can be adequately described by the label 'war-poet'. Alun Lewis (1915–44) of Aberdare enlisted in 1940, and his talents as a poet and short-story writer were forced to early maturity under the pressure of war and the pain of separation from his wife Gweno, to whom he was married in 1941. His short stories convey the frustrations of army life, often using Wales as an emotional touchstone. In the poems of *Raiders' Dawn* (1942) sexual passion is disturbingly interconnected with a sense of imminent violence, and the great themes of love and death came increasingly to dominate his work after he was posted to India in 1942. In the poems he wrote there, published in the ironically titled volume *Ha! Ha! Among the Trumpets* (1945), the certainties of Western culture are seen to be shaken by the encounter with an alien world.

The poetry of Alun Llywelyn-Williams (1913–88) is more assured in its conception of European civilization, which the experience of war tended, paradoxically, to reinforce. Born in Cardiff, Welsh was

Alun Llywelyn-Williams
from 'In Berlin – August 1945'

Sharp is the breeze; Heledd, do not shiver, do not weep;
take courage, hidden on the handy bed of the rubble,
as a gift for savouring the cigarette, for sucking the chocolate,
you can reach out your love to the lonely conqueror.
The night drips without mercy.
When will he come, when, when, the blue official,
his uniform spruce, his aloof good taste,
to sound his horn and start the crowd once more?
A gross, pompous city this has always been,
and fit to be ruined;
and have you heard, Heledd, – no, wounded Inge, –
the greedy eagle's fierce laughter,
have you seen, in his half-closed eyes,
the predestined image of all our frail cities?

(Translated by Joseph Clancy, *Twentieth Century Welsh Poems*)

very much his second language, and he is an interesting case of an
author who could very naturally have used English, but committed
himself to Welsh by an act of will. He took a detached view of the
Welsh tradition, however, feeling that it needed to encompass
urban experience, and with that aim he founded the magazine *Tir
Newydd* ('New Ground') in 1935. Much concerned with the forces
of change in modern life, his poetry nevertheless affirms a
humanistic belief in the healing power of art. His description of the
city of Berlin, which he saw with the occupying army at the end of
the war, draws on the early Welsh Heledd cycle to convey the
universality of the suffering caused by war.

10 Post-War Literature

New Welsh writing in the 1950s

Although some modernist features have already been noted in the Welsh literature of the first half of the century, it was in the 1950s that modernism really flourished in Welsh, taking on a distinctive character through association with religion and nationalism. A work which has affinities with the ironic self-critical modernism of T. S. Eliot is Kitchener Davies's long poem of 1952, *Sŵn y Gwynt sy'n Chwythu*, noted in the previous chapter. The impression of a fragmented personality in that poem is also apparent in T. Glynne Davies's *pryddest* of 1951 on the loss of the old hill-farms, 'Adfeilion' ('Ruins'), which blends nostalgia with surrealist imagery. The decline of the rural way of life was very obvious after the war, and is a major theme in the literature, for instance in the novels of W. Leslie Richards. But the Welsh modernism of the post-war period is more essentially concerned with renewal, both spiritual and national. The earliest manifestation of this new spirit was the Cadwgan Circle, a group of writers who met in the Rhondda home of J. Gwyn Griffiths during the war, seeking to follow contemporary trends in European culture. Three members of the group who have since made significant contributions to Welsh literature are Rhydwen Williams, Gareth Alban Davies, and the religious writer Pennar Davies, who first published in English under the pseudonym Davies Aberpennar, but chose to write his poetry and fiction in his second language.

The new modernism came to fruition with the publication of remarkable first volumes by three poets, Waldo Williams, Euros Bowen, and Bobi Jones. Of these, the best-known was Waldo Williams (1904–71), whose *Dail Pren* ('Leaves of a Tree') of 1956 was a long-overdue collection of poems going back to the thirties. Waldo was a committed pacifist whose idealism was inherited from his radical Baptist background in Pembrokeshire (he later became a Quaker), and at the core of his work are the poems written in response to the Second World War and the Korean War, when he was imprisoned for withholding his income tax. His poetry upholds the Romantic ideal of universal brotherhood, rooted in his experience of co-operation amongst the farmers of the Preseli Hills, which he took as the pattern of an ideal social order, as he declared in 'Preseli', written in protest against Ministry of Defence plans to take over the land. His greatest poem, 'Mewn Dau Gae' ('In Two

Waldo Williams
'Preseli'

Wall of my boyhood, Foel Drigarn, Carn Gyfrwy, Tal Mynydd,
Backing me in all independence of judgment,
And my floor from Y Witwg to Y Wern and down to Yr Efail
Where the sparks spurted that are older than iron.

And in the yards, on the hearths of my people –
Breed of wind, rain, and mist, of sword-flag and heather,
Wrestling with the earth and the sky and winning
And handing on the sun to their children, from their stooping.

Memory and symbol, a reaping party on their neighbour's hillside,
Four swaths of oats falling at every stroke,
And a single swift course, and while stretching their backs
Giant laughter to the clouds, a single peal of four voices.

My Wales, land of brotherhood, my cry, my creed,
Only balm for the world, its message, its challenge,
Pearl of the infinite hour held hostage by time,
Hope of the long journey on the short winding way.

This was my window, the harvesting and the shearing.
I beheld order in my palace there.
A roar, a ravening, is roaming the windowless forest.
Let us guard the wall against the beast, keep the well-spring free of the filth.

(Based on translation by Joseph Clancy, *Twentieth Century Welsh Poems*)

Fields') of 1956, is based on a vision of brotherhood which he had whilst working on a neighbour's farm as a boy. In one sense his traditionalist social ideals may seem to be at odds with his very modernist poetic style, but in fact his nationalism is creative rather than defensive, dependent on his belief in the power of the creative imagination to overcome material circumstances, a belief which is realized on a stylistic level in his bold use of imagery and symbolism.

Euros Bowen (1904–88) began to write poetry in earnest quite late in life, although there was a strong tradition in his family (his brother Geraint won the National Eisteddfod Chair in 1946 with a finely crafted poem in praise of the farmer). But after the publication in 1958 of his first collection, *Cerddi* ('Poems'), he produced a steady flow of volumes until his death. He experimented constantly with poetic form, and was the first to make extensive use of *cynghanedd* in free verse. His treatment of nature has a vivid impressionistic quality which reflects his interest in painting, but the sacramental interpretation is in keeping with his vocation as parish priest. Unlike Waldo Williams and Bobi Jones, his work has no overt political content, but he shares with them a reliance on the image as his essential medium of expression and an exultant Christian faith. The Resurrection is of crucial significance in the poetry of all three as a symbol of the triumph of the life-force, often represented by the season of spring (with political connotations for the Welsh nation), and stands in telling contrast to the obsession with death in the work of agnostic writers of the previous generation such as R. Williams Parry.

The new spirit of the post-war period is most clearly seen in the work of Bobi Jones, who represents better than any other writer the resurgence of the Welsh language. Born in Cardiff in 1929 into an English-speaking family, he learnt Welsh at school, taking a degree in the subject, and as critic, scholar, and above all creative writer, he has been one of the outstanding exponents of the language for over forty years. The fact that Welsh is, or was, his second language can even be seen to have been an advantage in his writing, for he uses it with an uninhibited freshness and has the passionate commitment of the convert. The experience of conversion is central to his evangelical Calvinism, which gives meaning and purpose to all his work, and perhaps partially accounts for his prodigious energy. His first collection of poetry, *Y Gân Gyntaf* ('The First Song'), was published in 1957, provoking both admiration and controversy by its exuberant and uncompromising style, and he has been a prolific and stimulating writer of poetry and fiction ever since. One of his most impressive, if daunting, achievements is the epic poem interpreting Welsh history, *Hunllef Arthur* ('Arthur's Nightmare') of 1986. Bobi Jones is a disciple of Saunders Lewis in many ways, not least in his broad cultural perspective which enables him to transcend British parochialism. Whilst Christian nationalism forms the ideological basis of his work, its constant emotional core has been his love for his wife Beti.

Bobi Jones
'A Little Monoglot Welsh Girl'

You ought to be lost as you swing over there
In a space within a foreign-speaking crowd, deaf, dumb,
Or at least be nursing a psychological stifling.
It isn't that way at all. You just chatter, because
It's your language that's the only one in the world.
It's the only one the evening speaks, and the hillside and the
    slide
And everyone who's around you, besides the unseen
Crowd that accompanies you everywhere
Like a secret family. You're an industry of fine babbling
And your countless wheels maintain play, –
The most solemn of callings. You're a revival with a
    thousand
Evangelists I hear in everything that's flying;
You're a lively halleluia. A millionaire in syllables –
Every life that's had being is speaking in you
And the language of the squirrel's in your ankles.
And when you renounce the frisking for a moment, and come
To break a word with us like a loaf – in our alabaster baskets
Where our sentences have been swept, in our cupboards
Of dreamwood where our arguments have been hung,
In our ditch's idleness, – to break a word like snow across us
Out of your monoglot cloud – what an eloquent honour is
    ours.

(Translated by Joseph Clancy, *Bobi Jones: Selected Poems*)

The 1950s was a period of great importance in the Welsh theatre, for in addition to the mature plays of Saunders Lewis discussed in the previous chapter, it was then that another major dramatist emerged with the publication in 1958 of *Two Plays* by John Gwilym Jones (1904–88). A writer whose intermittent career spans several periods, John Gwilym Jones had already made a notable contribution to Welsh modernist writing in 1946 with his collection of short stories, *Y Goeden Eirin* ('The Plum Tree'), using the stream of consciousness technique to reveal the gulf between outward conduct and inner life. Tensions within the family and their influence on the formation of personality are explored in all his major works, such as *Y Tad a'r Mab* ('The Father and the Son') in 1963 and his late novel *Tri Diwrnod ac Angladd* ('Three Days and a Funeral') of 1979. His vision is a sceptical humanist one, doubting all dogmas and stressing the universality of feelings and the value of human relationships, as seen in his unorthodox interpretation of the life and work of Morgan Llwyd, *Hanes Rhyw Gymro* ('The Story of a Certain Welshman'), published in 1964. As a dramatist the comparison with Saunders Lewis is inevitable, and although Lewis's work has greater range and intellectual depth, it is John Gwilym Jones who has represented the Welsh psyche most convincingly, knowing his people in a way which Lewis as an outsider never did. His characters are educated and articulate and yet deeply uncertain, heirs to a Nonconformity whose meaning has withered, leaving them caught in an existential predicament. No other Welsh writer has presented the anguish of modern life so powerfully, and it is a measure of his achievement that such essentially Welsh plays have been successful in translation in America and England.

The Welsh novel received new impetus in the 1950s with the emergence of Islwyn Ffowc Elis (b. 1924). The slate-quarrying novels had been essentially backward-looking, and no major novelist had yet taken on Daniel Owen's mantle as critic of contemporary society. Islwyn Ffowc Elis proved his mastery of the craft of prose with the publication in 1952 of a fine collection of essays, *Cyn Oeri'r Gwaed* ('Before the Blood Cools'), and made his name as a novelist with the immensely popular *Cysgod y Cryman* ('The Shadow of the Sickle') of 1953. That novel was undeniably modern in its theme of social change in a rural community, and yet its treatment of character is entirely conventional and it tends to avoid the implications of the radical issues which it raises (as can be seen by comparison with the similar novel by Emyr Humphreys, *A Man's Estate*). Elis sought greater psychological complexity in his next novel, a satirical portait of a group of Welsh intellectuals, *Ffenestri tua'r Gwyll* ('Windows towards the Dusk'), published in 1955, but the disappointment of his audience persuaded him to return to the rural setting in the following year with a sequel, *Yn ôl i Leifior* ('Back to Lleifior'). His nationalist sympathies are clear enough in those novels, and became overt in his powerful political satire of 1957, *Wythnos yng Nghymru Fydd* ('A Week in the Wales of the Future'). He subsequently produced several lighter novels in an attempt to create a wider readership for Welsh fiction. Islwyn Ffowc Elis's career can be seen as a case of unfulfilled promise, excessively governed by audience expectations, but nevertheless he must be credited with laying the foundations for the contemporary novel and establishing artistic standards in the neglected discipline of Welsh prose.

The second flowering of Anglo-Welsh literature

It is customary to refer to the generation of Anglo-Welsh writers who emerged after the Second World War as the second flowering, as distinct from the first generation from Caradoc Evans through to the writers of the thirties. The difference lies in attitudes towards Wales, the new generation being much more sympathetic towards nationalism and the Welsh language, tending to take a national rather than a regional perspective and to make less of a show of their Welshness, which suggests that they were writing for their own people rather than for the English. The change is due in large measure to the influence of Saunders Lewis and the nationalist fervour which resulted from the burning of the Bombing School in 1936, but the impact of the Second World War on rural Wales also contributed to the sense of crisis. A lead was given by two major writers who have dominated Welsh writing in English throughout the second half of this century, the poet R. S. Thomas and the novelist Emyr Humphreys, both of whom learnt Welsh as adults. The spirit of the new movement is reflected by the magazine *Dock Leaves* (later to become *The Anglo-Welsh Review*), founded in 1949 under the editorship of the poet Raymond Garlick with the aim of fostering contact between Welsh and Anglo-Welsh writers.

R. S. Thomas was born in Cardiff in 1913, but was brought up at Holyhead in Anglesey. He became a priest in the Church in Wales, and began learning Welsh seriously when he moved to the rural (but English-speaking) parish of Manafon in Montgomeryshire in 1942. Although he has fully mastered the language and published a good deal of prose in Welsh, he has never felt able to achieve the precision and intensity of language which distinguishes his English poetry. In 1954 he moved to the Welsh heartlands of the west, settling eventually at Aberdaron on the Llŷn peninsula. His first collection of poems, *The Stones of the Field*, was published in 1946, and since

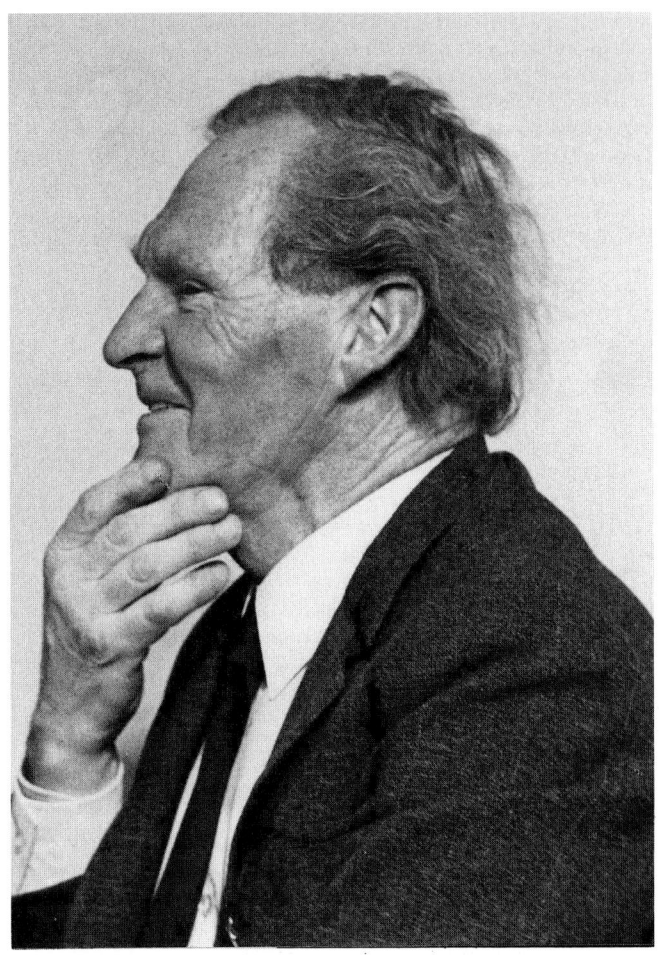

R. S. Thomas.

then he has produced a total of twenty-four volumes of poetry. His early work is principally concerned with his response to the hill farmers of Manafon (epitomized by the character Iago Prytherch), a mixture of revulsion and disappointment that they did not fulfil his romantic expectations, self-criticism of his own fastidiousness, and ultimately admiration for their enduring strength. The same sort of ambiguity is apparent in his treatment of Wales as a country, by turns detached and fiercely partisan. Welsh Wales seems to represent for Thomas a bulwark against the modern technological age, and he can be harshly critical of the Welsh themselves for failing to live up to that ideal.

R. S. Thomas
'Reservoirs'

There are places in Wales I don't go:
Reservoirs that are the subconscious
Of a people, troubled far down
With gravestones, chapels, villages even;
The serenity of their expression
Revolts me, it is a pose
For strangers, a watercolour's appeal
To the mass, instead of the poem's
Harsher conditions. There are the hills,
Too; gardens gone under the scum
Of the forests; and the smashed faces
Of the farms with the stone trickle
Of their tears down the hills' side.

Where can I go, then, from the smell
Of decay, from the putrefying of a dead
Nation? I have walked the shore
For an hour and seen the English
Scavenging among the remains
Of our culture, covering the sand
Like the tide and, with the roughness
Of the tide, elbowing our language
Into the grave that we have dug for it.

Emyr Humphreys.

The collection of religious poems, *H'm* (1972) marked a change of direction in Thomas's work (although there is a theological aspect to his treatment of nature in his earlier poems), and it is only recently that he has returned to the subject of Wales in his poetry, coinciding with some extreme statements on English immigration which have made him a notorious figure in Welsh politics. The major preoccupation of his later work is the exploration of the limitations of mankind's spiritual vision, the anguished searching for an absent God. It would be a mistake, however, to stereotype Thomas as either a Welsh nationalist or a religious poet. As the recently published *Collected Poems* shows (although it is far from complete), his work is much more wide-ranging, including some very evocative treatments of paintings and an important group of personal poems about his family. Whilst defiantly rooted in a Welsh context, his investigation of the spiritual crisis of our age, which continues in his latest collection, *Mass for Hard Times* (1992), is of far wider relevance, and his taut phrasing and the disturbing power of his imagery make him one of the greatest poets writing in English today.

Emyr Humphreys (b. 1919) was brought up in the Anglicized north-east of Wales, but learnt Welsh in the late thirties whilst studying at the University College of Wales, Aberystwyth, where he became a Welsh nationalist. Unlike R. S. Thomas, he did attempt to use his second language for his creative writing, publishing one of his early novels in equally successful English and Welsh versions in 1958, *A Toy Epic* and *Y Tri Llais* ('The Three Voices'), and he has also written film scripts in Welsh, but the confidence and subtlety of his English prose style was the decisive factor in his choice of medium for the bulk of his work. Nevertheless, the characters of much of his fiction are to be assumed to be speaking Welsh, and he has become a sympathetic but unsentimental interpreter of Welsh Wales both to its own people and to the English-speaking world. Emyr Humphreys has done valuable work as a poet, dramatist, and short-story writer, but his main creative energies have been in the field of the novel. Beginning in 1946 with *The Little Kingdom*, based on the burning of the Bombing School ten years earlier, he has published a total of eighteen novels, culminating with the series of seven entitled 'Bonds of Attachment' which was completed in 1991.

One of Emyr Humphreys's great strengths as a novelist is his inventive use of different narrative methods in order to convey the complexity of social interaction. As its Welsh title indicates, *A Toy*

Epic is narrated by the voices of three schoolboys, conveying the ways in which their lives are shaped by their cultural environment. *A Man's Estate* (1955) depicts the conflicting forces producing change in a rural community by alternating between the viewpoints of four contrasting characters. His finest single achievement is *Outside the House of Baal* (1965), which narrates the life of a Methodist minister by alternating between past and present, showing the failure of his Christian nationalist ideals and providing a view of the development of modern Wales. That novel can be seen as the germ of the more ambitious 'Bonds of Attachment' project, which has a much broader scope encompassing the variety and tensions within modern Welsh society. The central narrative thread is the life of Amy Parry, a journey which can be seen to represent the common experience of the Welsh people, from a radicalism born of poverty, through patriotism and socialism, ending in conformist affluence.

The fiction of Raymond Williams (1921–88) is comparable with that of Emyr Humphreys as an exploration of the socio-political forces at work in the lived experience of a particular place. Williams is of course best known as a highly influential cultural historian and guru of the New Left, but he has made an important contribution to the literature of the border with his trilogy of novels, *Border Country* (1960), *Second Generation* (1964), and *The Fight for Manod* (1979), drawing on his own upbringing in the village of Pandy in Monmouthshire and his experience of national and class borders arising from his academic career at Cambridge. His socialism was of a less materialistic kind than that which opposed nationalism between the wars, flexible enough to respond positively to the new Welsh consciousness. At the time of his death he was working on a panoramic fictional account of the history of his own region from the earliest human settlements, published posthumously in two volumes entitled *The People of the Black Mountains* (1989, 1990). In contrast to Bruce Chatwin's novel *On the Black Hill* (1982), which treats the border country of Radnorshire as a strange world set apart from the flow of history, the border in the work of Raymond Williams is at the centre of historical events and has a metaphorical significance which is relevant to the modern world as a whole.

It was in the 1960s that the second flowering of Anglo-Welsh literature reached its peak, when the mature works of R. S. Thomas and Emyr Humphreys were accompanied by the emergence of a new generation of poets, for whom a focus was provided by the magazine *Poetry Wales*, founded by Meic Stephens in 1965. The most fiercely political of these poets was Harri Webb (b. 1920), whose first collection, *The Green Desert*, was published in 1969, the year that the investiture of the Prince of Wales infuriated nationalists. John Tripp (1927–86) was more concerned with the sense of disinheritance, and his commitment to Welsh ideals was tinged by an ironic awareness of his own ambiguous status as an English-speaker from Cardiff. A poet who has done much to narrow the gap between the two literatures of Wales is Anthony Conran (b. 1931). A distinguished translator of Welsh poetry (his *Penguin Book of Welsh Verse* of 1967 has had considerable influence on Anglo-Welsh poets), he has drawn extensively on Welsh models in his own work, as for instance in taking Aneirin's *Gododdin* as the basis for his elegy for Welsh soldiers killed in the Falklands War. Of course, not all the poetry of this period was on overtly national themes. John Ormond (1923–90), for example, was a highly individual voice, and yet still distinctively Anglo-Welsh in

Harri Webb
'Israel'

Listen, Wales. Here was a people
Whom even you could afford to despise,
Growing nothing, making nothing,
Belonging nowhere, a people
Whose sweat-glands had atrophied,
Who lived by their wits,
Who lived by playing the violin
(A lot better, incidentally
Than you ever played the harp).
And because they were such a people
They went like lambs to the slaughter.

But some survived (yes, listen closer now)
And these are a different people,
They have switched off Mendelssohn
And tuned in to Maccabeus.
The mountains are red with their blood,
The deserts are green with their seed.
Listen, Wales.

his concern for his family background in the Swansea region. The poetry and lyrical short stories of Leslie Norris are typical of much Anglo-Welsh writing in locating Welshness in childhood experience. The adult world of Norris's work is much more cosmopolitan, as is that of Raymond Garlick (*A Sense of Europe*, 1968), Roland Mathias, Gwyn Williams (another fine translator of Welsh poetry), and the novelist, poet and playwright Dannie Abse, who participates in two minority cultures by virtue of his Cardiff Jewish family background.

Recent writing in Welsh
The most remarkable feature of Welsh poetry over the last quarter century is the revival of the strict-metre tradition towards the end of the sixties. Although they never died out altogether, the strict metres had fallen somewhat out of fashion around the middle of the century. Based initially on the work of the *beirdd gwlad* (folk poets), their revival was no doubt part of the international tendency towards traditionalism in many fields, but it also had a specifically Welsh significance in the context of the rise of popular protest movements in defence of the language, since *cynghanedd* was felt to be a uniquely Welsh poetic form and its emphatic rhythms were a highly effective medium for political propaganda. The widespread

Alan Llwyd.

folk tradition from which the revival sprang is best represented by the remarkable Cilie family of Cardiganshire, descendants of Jeremiah Jones (1855–1902). Dic Jones (b. 1934), one of the finest modern exponents of the strict metres, is a product of the Cilie circle, and continues to uphold the ideal of the poet as skilled craftsman entertaining and celebrating his community. But such traditionalism could not take in the new political radicalism of the time. This is most forcefully expressed in the work of Gerallt Lloyd Owen (b. 1944), whose 1972 collection *Cerddi'r Cywilydd* ('Poems of the Disgrace') was a scathing response to the investiture of the Prince of Wales in 1969. On the seven-hundredth anniversary of the death of the last native prince of Wales, Llywelyn ap Gruffudd, in 1982, Owen won the chair of the National Eisteddfod with an inspired *awdl* relating the event to the condition of modern Wales.

Strict-metre poetry has continued to flourish up to the present day, and its contemporaneity gives the lie to the once common claim that such traditional modes are an anachronism in the modern world. The most successful metrical form is the four-line *englyn*, of which an example is given below. Outstanding among the poets produced by the revival is Alan Llwyd (b. 1948), who has

Alan Llwyd

'Tranc y Cof'

(Wedi Marwolaeth Saunders Lewis)

Mae ein Cof fel ogof laith, – ond di-swn
Yw'r atseinio hirfaith
O'i mewn, lle clywem unwaith
Lenwi'r hollt gan lanw'r iaith.

'The Demise of the Memory'
(After the Death of Saunders Lewis)

Our Memory is like a damp cave, but soundless
Is the long echoing
Inside it, where we once heard
The gap filled by the tide of the language.

done a great deal to promote Welsh poetry as editor of the magazine *Barddas*, founded in 1976. Entirely dedicated to the profession of poetry, he has produced eleven volumes since 1971, employing the strict metres with astonishing virtuosity and extending the range of *cynghanedd* in free verse. Between the two poles of his monoglot upbringing in the Welsh heartland of Llŷn and his experience of urban life in Swansea, Alan Llwyd's work adopts a conservative Christian viewpoint which places the condition of modern Wales in the context of the crisis of human civilization in the twentieth century.

The difference between strict and free metres in recent Welsh poetry is more than just one of form. Free-metre poetry has a broader scope, both in subject-matter and tone. The poets have a less exalted conception of their role than exponents of the strict metres, and self-deprecatory humour is much more evident in their work. Although generally sympathetic towards nationalism and deeply concerned about the future of the Welsh language, as anyone writing in a minority language must be, their attitude is less defensive than that of more traditionalist poets. Pre-eminent among free-metre poets since the 1960s is Gwyn Thomas (b. 1936), a scholar who is now professor of Welsh at Bangor. In his academic work Thomas has sought to make the Welsh literary tradition accessible to the general reader, and his poetry has a similar aim, dealing with contemporary life in a direct and often colloquial style, whilst also drawing to great effect on a wide range of mythology. As is apparent in the titles of his first two collections, *Chwerwder yn y Ffynhonnau* ('Bitterness in the Wells') and *Y Weledigaeth Haearn* ('The Iron Vision'), published in 1962 and 1965 respectively, his early poetry was a response to the destructive forces of an impersonal technological world. That harsh vision was subsequently tempered by his genial treatment of the idiosyncratic world of children, and his mature work offers a balanced and deeply humane view of life.

A very welcome development over the last two decades is the emergence of a number of fine female poets. The male-dominated bardic tradition had previously tended to preclude women from poetry, and their contribution in this century has been much greater in the field of prose fiction. But such barriers were broken down with the rise of the feminist movement, and Welsh poetry has been considerably enriched by new voices, especially those of Nesta Wyn Jones and Menna Elfyn, the latter a committed feminist whose challenging views on radical issues are expressed in images of striking originality. Another challenge to established tradition is the series provocatively entitled 'Y Beirdd Answyddogol' ('The Unofficial Poets'), published by Y Lolfa, uneven in quality but often stimulating, having close links with the very lively Welsh rock music scene and putting a healthy emphasis on the performance of poetry. The opposing poles of traditionalism and radicalism certainly reflect real divisions in Welsh politics and society, but it would be a mistake to see Welsh poets as irreconcilably divided into opposing camps, since the two tendencies are combined in the work of excellent young poets, such as Iwan Llwyd, as well as older ones such as Bryan Martin Davies. The variety and tensions within contemporary Welsh poetry are surely evidence of its ability to encompass the wide range of modern experience both within and beyond Wales.

The absence of a strong tradition has been both a weakness and a strength for the Welsh novel in recent years. Novelists lack the firm basis of inherited forms and social status which Welsh poets possess, but on the other hand they have had the freedom to develop new and more challenging modes of writing. The comforting genre of the historical novel has of course retained its appeal, and the conventional virtues of a well-told story are evident in the contemporary novels of Alun Jones and Eigra Lewis Roberts, who is very much in the Kate Roberts mould, whilst Jane Edwards has gone further in exploring the psychological problems of middle-class life. But the most significant development has been those novels which call into question cultural assumptions and undermine accepted notions of literary decorum.

The taboo subject of sexuality was first broached in explicit terms in the 1960s in the work of John Rowlands, an academic whose encouraging criticism has since been invaluable to a new generation of Welsh novelists. Perhaps the most dedicated of that generation is Aled Islwyn, whose novel *Sarah Arall* ('Another Sarah'), of 1980, explores the condition of anorexia and its associated sexual problems in poetic prose of great psychological subtlety. The failure of nationalism in the decade culminating in the disastrous referendum of 1979 is the subject of his *Cadw'r Chwedlau'n Fyw* ('Keeping the Stories Alive'), published in 1984. The disillusionment of the post-referendum period is most vividly captured in Angharad Tomos's bitterly ironic novel, *Yma o Hyd* ('Still Here'), published in 1985 and based on her experience of imprisonment as a language activist. Urban experience has become much more prominent in the Welsh novel, at its most sordidly shocking in Siôn Eirian's *Bob yn y Ddinas* ('Bob in the City') of 1979. That novel is firmly located in the city of Cardiff, but Wil Roberts's Kafkaesque *Bingo!* (1984) has an entirely impersonal urban setting. Roberts went on to produce a major work of postmodernist fiction, *Y Pla* (1987, available in English translation as *The Pestilence*), set in fourteenth-century Wales but defying all the conventions of the historical novel in order to present a disturbingly raw and violent image of medieval society grounded in a Marxist view of the historical process. The Welsh novel seems at present to be developing in various postmodernist directions, mostly with political significance close to the surface, such as Robin Llywelyn's lively fantasy, *Seren Wen ar Gefndir Gwyn* ('A White Star on a White Background'), published in 1992, and Mihangel Morgan's *Dirgel Ddyn* ('Hidden Man') of 1993, two products of the National Eisteddfod's prose competition.

A younger contemporary of John Gwilym Jones who made an equally important contribution to Welsh drama in the sixties and seventies was Gwenlyn Parry (1932–91). Eschewing the naturalist drama of Saunders Lewis, his work shows the influence of the Absurdist movement in European theatre, most notably in *Saer Doliau* ('The Dollmaker') of 1966, an enigmatic allegory about man's religious faith. In his later work, such as *Y Ffin* ('The Border') and *Y Twr* ('The Tower'), published in 1973 and 1978 respectively, dramatic situations are given powerful symbolic resonance. Like his English-language counterparts such as Ewart Alexander, much of Gwenlyn Parry's writing has been for television, in which he developed a fine ear for dialogue but expended his energy on popular material such as the soap opera *Pobol y Cwm*. The same is true of a number of younger dramatists since the establishment in 1982 of the Welsh television channel, S4C, which has made it possible for Welsh writers to earn a living from their work for the first time since the Middle Ages. It is interesting to note that Wil Roberts, who earns his living as a scriptwriter, still uses prose fiction as a medium for the exploration of profounder themes undictated by commercial concerns. The most stimulating Welsh drama in recent years has been non-literary events, produced by companies such as *Brith Gof* and *Moving Being* who combine words with music and dance.

Gillian Clarke.

Recent writing in English

The diversification of Welsh writing in English since the 1970s has made the term 'Anglo-Welsh' seem somewhat redundant. Whereas writers of the Second Flowering objected to being described as Anglo-Welsh because it seemed to imply a dilution of their Welshness, those of this latest phase object to having the scope of their work circumscribed by a term which places them in a specifically national context. Of course, there are writers who continue to regard Welsh-speaking Wales as a social ideal, such as the poets Gillian Clarke and Nigel Jenkins. Brought up in Cardiff, Gillian Clarke (b. 1937) has made her home in the rural west, and writes with profound sympathy for the world of nature, linking its rhythms to those of women's lives. Her recent long poem about her memories of her father, 'The King of Britain's Daughter' (1993), is based on the legend of Branwen from the *Mabinogi*. But on the whole, there has been a reaction against the historically-based nationalism exemplified by the early work of R. S. Thomas. Influenced by the work of labour historians such as Gwyn Alf Williams, new writers have focused on their post-industrial environment, with a strong sense of the ways in which conditions of work have shaped people's lives.

The poetry of Robert Minhinnick (b. 1952) presents a sharply observed and menacing image of the decay of late capitalist society in his native region of Bridgend. Ecological awareness and sympathy for the exploited and marginalized are far more important in his work than any nationalistic concerns. That is not to say that such writing is any less Welsh than the work of writers who foreground their national identity. The sense of place and identification with its people are distinctive, as is the evocative descriptive power, which recalls the work of Glyn Jones. Another outstanding poet writing above all about the people of south Wales is Tony Curtis (b. 1946), who uses colloquial speech forms with moving effect. The prominence of the elegy in Curtis's work, and in that of other Anglo-Welsh poets, raises the interesting possibility that the centrality of that essentially social genre in the Welsh tradition has been taken over into English-language writing in Wales. Bilingualism, or alternatively linguistic divisions, can certainly be seen to have stimulated an interest in the nature of language itself, its eccentricities and infinite productivity, as in the zestfully experimental poems of Peter Finch (b. 1947), an author who has done much to promote avant-garde poetics in Wales. As already seen in Welsh, women writers have played a much more prominent part in recent English-language writing, leading to a welcome broadening of its thematic range. In addition to Gillian Clarke, and amongst several others, the poets Ruth Bidgood and Sheenagh Pugh deserve mention, as does the short-story writer Glenda Beagan.

The decline of Wales's industries has lead to a spate of historical novels about the early development of the industrial communities, most notably the highly popular works of Alexander Cordell, beginning with *Rape of the Fair Country* (1959), a vividly romanticized account of the Chartist movement in Monmouthshire. But recent fiction in English has not turned away from the realities of post-industrial Wales. The novels and short stories of Alun Richards and Ron Berry in the sixties and seventies portray the valleys of south Wales no longer beset by the material hardships of the Depression period, but in a state of spiritual decay as their industrial base is eroded. The humour which continues to alleviate the pain in their work is much less apparent in contemporary writing, such as Christopher Meredith's account of the closure of a Gwent steel works, *Shifts* (1988), and the grim portrait of urban isolation in Duncan Bush's *Glass Shot* (1991), a *tour de force* in which the author's political anger at the treatment of the miners during the 1984 strike is concealed behind the persona of a rapist. These accounts of social disintegration are paralleled in the theatre by the plays of Edward Thomas, the most forceful of contemporary English-language dramatists.

The literature of Wales has always been a vital factor in the Welsh people's sense of national identity, expressing their allegiance to the

Gillian Clarke
'Blaen Cwrt'

You ask how it is. I will tell you.
There is no glass. The air spins in
The stone rectangle. We warm our hands
With apple wood. Some of the smoke
Rises against the ploughed, brown field
As a sign to our neighbours in the
Four folds of the valley that we are in.
Some of the smoke seeps through the stones
Into the barn where it curls like fern
On the walls. Holding a thick root
I press my bucket through the surface
Of the water, lift it brimming and skim
The leaves away. Our fingers curl on
Enamel mugs of tea, like ploughmen.
The stones clear in the rain
Giving their colours. It's not easy.
There are no brochure blues or boiled sweet
Reds. All is ochre and earth and cloud-green
Nettles tasting sour and the smells of moist
Earth and sheep's wool. The wattle and daub
Chimney hood has decayed away, slowly
Creeping to dust, chalking the slate
Floor with stories. It has all the first
Necessities for a high standard
Of civilised living: silence inside
A circle of sound, water and fire,
Light on uncountable miles of mountain
From a big, unpredictable sky,
Two rooms, waking and sleeping,
Two languages, two centuries of past
To ponder on, and the basic need
To work hard in order to survive.

past and their will to survive as a separate nation in spite of political setbacks. This has never been more true than at the present time, when the linguistic communities which have always nurtured the literature are under severe pressure. The existence of literatures in the two languages is an inevitable reflex of the colonial condition of modern Wales, and the tensions between them, and also within each one, give voice to the multiplicity of viewpoints amongst this fragmented people. As it has done in the past, the state of crisis adds an urgency to Welsh writing which has a wider significance in the context of attempts by other peoples to preserve their distinctive identities under threat from the bland uniformity of Anglo-American culture. On the other hand, it is a healthy sign that a number of younger contemporary writers are less obsessed with the predicament of the nation and its language than their immediate predecessors, preferring to deal with wider issues from a Welsh viewpoint. But in whichever language they write, the perspective deriving from a particular place and its past is crucial. As Saunders Lewis memorably declared, 'Civilization must be more than an abstraction. It must have a local habitation and a name. Here, its name is Wales.'

Further Reading

General

Historical and cultural background is provided by two companion volumes in this series by J. Graham Jones, *The History of Wales* (1990), and Trefor M. Owen, *The Customs and Traditions of Wales* (1991). On the language see Janet Davies, *The Welsh Language* (1993). The Celtic context of Welsh language and literature is surveyed in Glanville Price (ed.), *The Celtic Connection* (1992). Emyr Humphreys, *The Taliesin Tradition* (1983), explores the significance of literature for the Welsh identity. The first two volumes of *A Guide to Welsh Literature* (1976, 1979; revised edn of vol.I 1992) contain authoritative accounts of all aspects of early and medieval literature. On Arthurian literature see R. Bromwich, A. O. H. Jarman and B. F. Roberts (eds), *The Arthur of the Welsh* (1991). Sioned Davies, *The Four Branches of the Mabinogi* (1993), is an excellent introduction to the art of the medieval story-teller. The best survey of Welsh humanism is R. Geraint Gruffydd, 'The Renaissance and Welsh literature', in G. Williams and R. O. Jones (eds.), *The Celts and the Renaissance* (1990). Prys Morgan, *The Eighteenth-century Renaissance* (1981), is a stimulating study of the neo-classical movement. Essential works on Welsh writing in English are Glyn Jones, *The Dragon Has Two Tongues* (1968); Anthony Conran, *The Cost of Strangeness* (1982); and M. Wynn Thomas, *Internal Difference* (1992). Also useful is Roland Mathias, *Anglo-Welsh Literature: An Illustrated History* (1987). The 'Writers of Wales' series contains introductory monographs on most major authors. An invaluable work of reference is Meic Stephens (ed.), *The Oxford Companion to the Literature of Wales* (1986). For detailed studies in Welsh and English see the comprehensive bibliography in two volumes, *Llyfryddiaeth Llenyddiaeth Gymraeg* (1976, 1993). The recently published *A Bibliographical Guide to Twenty-Four Modern Anglo-Welsh Writers* (1994) compiled by John Harris is another useful reference work.

Texts and Translations

Three classics of the early poetic tradition are available in parallel-text editions in the 'Welsh Classics' series: A. O. H. Jarman,

Aneirin: Y Gododdin (1988); Rachel Bromwich, *Dafydd ap Gwilym: A Selection of Poems* (1982); Dafydd Johnston, *Iolo Goch: Poems* (1993). The most authoritative work on the early medieval *englynion* is Jenny Rowland, *Early Welsh Saga Poetry* (1990). Translations of early and medieval poetry are available in Gwyn Williams, *The Burning Tree* (1956); Joseph Clancy, *The Earliest Welsh Poetry* (1970), and *Medieval Welsh Lyrics* (1965); and Richard Loomis and Dafydd Johnston, *Medieval Welsh Poems* (1992); whilst *The Oxford Book of Welsh Verse in English* (1977) and Tony Conran's *Welsh Verse* (1986) contain translations from all periods, the latter accompanied by a substantial and stimulating introduction. Two neglected aspects of the bardic tradition are revealed in parallel-text editions by Dafydd Johnston, *Medieval Welsh Erotic Poetry* (1991), and *Poets' Grief* (1993). The medieval prose tales are available in an admirable translation by Gwyn Jones and Thomas Jones, *The Mabinogion* (revised edn 1974).

The most substantial collection of modern poetry in translation is Joseph Clancy's *Twentieth Century Welsh Poems* (1982). Clancy has also translated selections of the poetry of Gwyn Thomas, *Living a Life* (1982), Bobi Jones, *Selected Poems* (1987), and Saunders Lewis, *Selected Poems* (1993), and of Kate Roberts's fiction, *The World of Kate Roberts* (1991). The best introduction to the work of Saunders Lewis is Alun R. Jones and Gwyn Thomas (eds), *Presenting Saunders Lewis* (1983), which contains translations of three of his plays and much of his poetry. Useful anthologies of Welsh writing in English are: Raymond Garlick and Roland Mathias (eds), *Anglo-Welsh Poetry 1480–1980* (1984); Meic Stephens (ed.), *The Bright Field* (1991); Alun Richards (ed.), *The Penguin Book of Welsh Short Stories* (1976; revised selection 1991); and John Davies (ed.), *The Green Bridge* (1988).

Index

141